Known across social media as 'the pasta queen', Carmela is passionate about pasta. Initially venturing into a food career through social media channels, she has a wide following of her food blog, videos and regular posts of recipes, tips and all things pasta. She is an established Italian cookery writer, teacher and restaurateur. Her first book, *Southern Italian Family Cooking* was published in 2014 and was a resounding success, focusing on *cucina povera*, peasant style cooking. Whilst Carmela still teaches some small classes from her family kitchen, she also demonstrates and teaches in London Restaurants and at corporate events and food festivals. Supper clubs and pop-up restaurants provide an opportunity to showcase her recipes and are a regular sell-out.

Born in the UK, but with parents from Puglia and Molise, Carmela is Italian at heart. As a busy mum of four children, she understands that food sometimes needs to be quick and practical. Her recipes are designed to be flexible and accessible to all, but with a hint of adventure through some more unusual ingredients.

Her skill in making beautiful pasta is remarkable. Stripes, spots and delicate herbs all feature across a range of shapes. This is what she is most passionate about and what she loves to do. To sum up Carmela she has a love of Italian food, seasonal ingredients and simple cooking but throughout her dishes you will always feel the passion and dedication shown through her knowledge and understanding of pasta. Be prepared to fall in love with the pasta from Carmela's kitchen.

Other titles

———

Southern Italian Family Cooking
A Lebanese Feast
Delicious Gluten-Free Baking
Everyday Lebanese Cooking
Patisserie
The Healthy Slow Cooker Cookbook
Mediterranean Cooking for Diabetics

A PASSION FOR PASTA

CARMELA SOPHIA SERENO

ROBINSON

ROBINSON

First published in Great Britain in 2017
by Robinson

3 5 7 9 10 8 6 4 2

A CIP catalogue record for this book
is available from the British Library.

ISBN: 978-1-47213-755-5

Designed and typeset in Agenda by
Andrew Barron @ thextension

Printed in Italy

Robinson
An imprint of
Little, Brown Book Group
Carmelite House
50 Victoria Embankment
London EC4Y 0DZ

An Hachette UK Company
www.hachette.co.uk

www.littlebrown.co.uk

A pasta dream come true.

Love to my husband James for his continued support & my four children who continue to inspire me – Rocco, Natalia, Santino and Chiara.

Baci sempre x

VALLE
D'AOSTA

PIEMONTE

Torino

LIGURIA

Genova

LOMBARDIA

Milano

Verona

TRENTINO-
ALTO ADIGE

Bolzano

VENETO

Venezia

FRIULI-
VENEZIA
GIULIA

Trieste

Bologna

EMILIA-ROMAGNA

Firenze

TOSCANA

MARCHE

Perugia

UMBRIA

Italy

Pescara

ABRUZZO

Roma

LAZIO

MOLISE

Foggia

Napoli

CAMPANIA

Bari

PUGLIA

Sassari

BASILICATA

Taranto

SARDEGNA

Cagliari

CALABRIA

Palermo

Messina

SICILIA

Catania

CONTENTS

1 INTRODUCTION

Regional cooking in Italy **2**

What is pasta? **5**

A history of pasta **7**

2 PASTA MAKING

How to cook and
store pasta **10**

How to make pasta
by hand **12**

Making pasta for filling **16**

Making unfilled
pasta shapes **22**

Colouring pasta **31**

Making gluten-free
pasta **40**

3 RECIPES BY REGION

Abruzzo **44**

Aosta Valley **54**

Basilicata **64**

Calabria **74**

Campania **84**

Emilia Romagna **94**

Friuli-Venezia Giulia **104**

Lazio **114**

Le Marche **124**

Liguria **134**

Lombardy **144**

Molise **154**

Piedmont **164**

Puglia **174**

Sardinia **184**

Sicily **194**

Trentino-Alto Adige **204**

Tuscany **214**

Umbria **224**

Veneto **234**

Stockists of Italian
ingredients **244**

Index **246**

1 INTRODUCTION

REGIONAL COOKING IN ITALY

It's impossible to think of Italian food without pasta being at the forefront of your mind. Imagine trying to live a life without pasta? For an Italian it would be like living a life without love and passion. It's not possible, is it?

The Italian kitchen is central to the hearts and minds of all Italian families; cooking connects you to your past. Growing up in our family home, pasta was more or less a daily meal, served at least five times a week. As young children my sister and I would love a bowl of *brodo* (soup or broth) with *pastina* (tiny pasta), or a simple warming bowl of pasta *e piseli* (with peas).

Pasta showcases the simplicity of Italian cooking along with its ease, affordability and flavour. No need for fast food when pasta *secca* (dried) can be cooked with a simple carbonara sauce and served within 15 minutes. I am an absolute pasta lover, and I'm not going to hide this fact one bit. I'm

▲ My father's village, Castellucio Vallmaggiore in the province of Foggia, Puglia.

passionate about making pasta by hand, experimenting with colouring techniques, shapes, and the various flours and combination of flavourings we can use to infuse what is an incredibly simple dough. With so many varieties of shapes and sauce combinations to choose from, I could quite easily eat this most amazing carbohydrate daily and never get bored. A simple dish of pasta that allows you to pick up a fork and indulge with a glass of full-bodied *vino rosso*: life doesn't get much better than that, does it?

My roots are in the south of Italy from the regions of Puglia and Molise. In Molise my mum's family are from the village of Oratino in the province of Campobasso, and from Puglia, my dad's side of the family are from Castelluccio Valmaggiore in Foggia province. I'm choosing to take my influences, along with the mantra of *cucina povera* (peasant cooking), on this mouth-watering journey with me. My own heritage is vital in my journey of discovery. Eating within the seasons is key, as well as using the best of what the seasons have to offer: fresh ingredients are vital as this ensures maximum flavour, an abundance of fruit and vegetables along with beautiful fresh seafood, fish and meat.

Growing up in a north Bedfordshire village was a blessing. The main town of Bedford is known as *Little Italy*, as this is where many of the Italian migrants from Southern Italy, including my family, settled in the late 1950s. I was lucky to grow up on a farm with my younger sister Daniela. My

▲ Buffalo mozzarella is a mozzarella made from the milk of the domestic Italian water buffalo. It is traditionally produced in Campania.

parents used to tend to their vast allotment, whilst chasing the goats then milking them, and collecting eggs from the rowdiest chickens on the block. My mother, Solidea, would make the most fantastic cheese using the fresh goat's milk. We actually had a cheese room in our house adjacent to my bedroom, and as a child I remember the pungent smell wafting through the house on a warm day, sometimes not that pleasing as you can imagine. Mum would sell the cheese to local Italian delis in Bedford in the early 1990s, as well as unpasteurised goat's milk – sometimes the milk would still be warm. Clearly, the laws changed and this practice was soon stopped, but to our advantage really as it meant we had the full benefit of Mum's cheese. Late summer, Mum would make the best red velvet passata in the world, using my father Rocco's fabulous Italian tomatoes along with a pinch of salt and fresh basil. Eggs would be taken to my grandmother (nonna) Carmela's house along with a huge assortment of fresh vegetables weekly. Nonna Carmela would make an arrangement of filled egg pasta using *farina doppio zero* ('00' flour) as well as our staple cicatelli and orecchiette pasta using *semola di grano duro* (wheat semolina). Nonna would share the homemade pasta equally with our family and my father's siblings. The vegetables from the allotment she would blanch and use to stock her freezer, giving some to her neighbour opposite who provided her with freshly caught eels from time to time. What this lady doesn't know about *cucina povera* isn't worth knowing. *Cucina povera* cooking echoes the simplicity of wonderful seasonal ingredients and produce paired with extras from the larder and fridge. Although in essence known as 'peasant cooking' or 'poor people's food', in my opinion this is the only way to cook and eat in Italy.

With twenty individual regions in Italy, you can only imagine how diverse the cooking is, from strongly held family recipes passed down through generations to classic regional dishes. The passion and strength of each region has an incredibly strong influence on its food, with each believing their dish is superior to the next region or even the next village within the same province. When it comes to pasta, each region specialises in its own unique signature shape and medley of sauces.

In my opinion the exact regionality of a dish isn't so important because they differ so much. Puglia is famous for *orecchiette con cime di rape* (little ears with turnip tops), but in our village, orecchiette is served with a heavy meat-based tomato sauce. In Campobasso my mum has vivid memories of Nonno Angelo, her father, adding red wine to pasta just before serving it. This pasta dish is called *La Tassa*. It tends to be made with a simple short pasta like penne, cicatelli or cavatelli and is normally served before the antipasti. Cook the pasta in a pan of boiling salted water, remembering to keep the pasta *al dente* (with a bite) and drain, reserving a ladle of the starchy pasta water. Mix the pasta, water and a small amount of red wine together, stir well and serve in small bowls. The pasta water helps to emulsify the dish. Only a small bowl per person is needed as this is not an actual part of the meal; it is merely a taster, a mouthful or two suffices. No cheese is added, keeping this dish very simple and in keeping with *cucina povera* cooking.

If pasta is cooked correctly it makes for the most mouth-watering meal anytime of the day. In *A Passion for Pasta*, I have included regional pasta dishes from as far north as Valle D'Aosta to the tip of the spicy Calabrian toe in the south, a combination of different and varied pasta shapes together with perfect sauce combinations. A few key points follow, which will help you to cook and serve a variety of dishes with confidence. Please join me in an Italian journey of discovery.

WHAT IS PASTA?

Nothing says Italy like its food, and nothing says Italian food like 'pasta', or in the words of Federico Fellini, 'Life is a combination of magic and pasta'.

The meaning of pasta is 'simple dough' – an unleavened dough of wheat and water. A simple classification into the two main groups of dried and fresh doesn't do justice to the massive array of shapes, sizes, colours and flavours available.

Found on most supermarket and deli shelves, pasta *secca* (dried) uses a blend of durum wheat semolina (*semola di grano duro)* and water. Mass-produced Italian dried pasta must be made with 100 per cent durum wheat flour; it has an excellent shelf life and can offer you the perfect meal in a matter of minutes. The simplest of sauces can be made whilst the pasta is happily bubbling away. My larder is stocked to the brim with a variety of dried pasta shapes, enabling me to rustle up a family meal incredibly quickly, and most of the time on demand!

As an alternative to durum wheat, '00' flour (*doppio zero, farina di grano tenero*) is my preference for egg-based pasta *fresca* (fresh pasta). Flour in Italy is graded due to its coarseness from very fine 000, with all traces of wheatgerm removed, through to 00, 0, 1, 2, 3, 4, becoming coarser and with less wheatgerm removed: 000 resembles a very fine talcum powder whereas 4 is verging on wholemeal. For pasta making, 00 flour is the ideal choice every time, though a combination of both durum wheat flour and 00 can also be used to give variation in colour and texture.

I like to ask my students, 'How many pasta shapes do you think there are?' The answer is invariably in the range of fifteen to maybe forty shapes. They are surprised to learn that there are over six hundred shapes of pasta available in Italy, from the famous and widely used penne, farfalle and spaghetti to some of the lesser known such as the incredibly delicious strozzapreti, bigoli, chitarra and gigli. It's not uncommon for the same shape to have different names across regions of Italy: the tagliatelle of the north is the fettuccine of Rome and what I call cicatelli someone else will call cavatelli. You would be forgiven for being a little confused!! Most factory-made pasta is extruded through a copper mould and cut to a specific shape before drying. Short ziti, penne or rigatoni that have ridges imbedded into them are called *rigate*. The ridges provide the pasta with a surface to which the sauce will cling. This is my favourite; I adore the ridges as opposed to a smoother shorter pasta. For the purist, specific shapes are meant for specific sauces – but there's no harm in experimenting!

Regional traditions and preferences can be seen across the country. The north of Italy tends to consume more rice and polenta than the south. However, when they come to make pasta they use '00' flour and eggs to give a richer pasta than in the drier plains of the south, where durum wheat and water is the preferred option. Veneto is well known for its *Bigoli con coniglio* (thick spaghetti with rabbit), Sicilia for *Pasta alla Norma* (pasta with aubergine), Abruzzo for *Pasta alla chitarra* (*chitarra* meaning guitar), and Campagnia for penne with a simple tomato sauce – seemingly endless possibilities to make your mouth water.

Fresh vs dried?

Many would assume that fresh is best. Whilst filled pasta such as ravioli, agnolotti and tortellini definitely needs to be fresh, in all other recipes, dried pasta would make the ideal choice. You will notice the difference in good-quality dried pasta, so use a reputable brand. No shop-own-brands please! Don't be limited by what your local supermarket is able to offer.

Search out an Italian deli or look online (see page 244) for a new shape or two to fall in love with. We all have our favourites when sitting around our family table. My problem is I, like so many, find it a challenge to choose!

This photograph makes my heart beat that little bit faster. It represents the roots of my pasta passion, built on the foundation of the art and simplicity of the *cucina povera* way of cooking. Two ladies are making orecchiette in the back streets of Bari, Puglia. For so many years this has been a hidden gem, a secret of the south. Nowadays tourists search it out as a living history of the traditions and authentic manner of making pasta. Whilst the days of grandmother, mother and daughter working together in the streets to make orecchiette to sell to passers-by and local eateries are gone, you will still find nonnas making pasta to feed their families, drying these delicate little ears on racks outside their houses in the dry, intense heat of Puglia.

A HISTORY OF PASTA

Did Marco Polo Bring Pasta to Italy?

There are stories that Marco Polo (1254–1324), a Venetian traveller, discoverer and explorer, brought pasta back to Italy via China. Whilst reminiscent of Sir Walter Raleigh bringing potatoes to Queen Elizabeth, alas there is no truth in the tale; it is but a myth. Pasta was being made in Italy when Polo visited China, and in fact many years before his birth.

In the Middle Ages, pasta was eaten by the Arabs who ruled Sicily at the time. There are also suggestions that the ancient Romans in the first century AD ate pasta and that ancient Greeks consumed a version of lasagne. The ancestors of the Italians (the Etruscans) made drawings depicting food that looked like pasta, even including drawings of instruments used to make and cut the dough.

An Arabic traveller who settled in Sicily in 1154 described delicate strings made from flour and water, now known to us as spaghetti. The will of Ponzio Baestone, a Genoan soldier, shows he requested 'Bariscella peina de macarone' – a small basket full of macaroni. His will was dated 1279, thirteen years before Marco Polo returned from China.

By the 1300s, dried pasta was very popular for its long shelf life and high nutritional value, making it an ideal choice for long ship voyages and other journeys. There is evidence of Etruscan Romans making pasta from durum wheat, which is still used to produce pasta today. It was called *lagane* and, like its modern-day namesake *lasagne,* was dried in sheets to preserve its life until it was needed for cooking.

Pasta did not become an important part of a meal in Italy until the sixteenth century. It was a luxury item because the special durum wheat needed to make it had to be imported from Sicily or Puglia, which made it expensive. Until the eighteenth century, poorer people in Italy mainly ate a diet based on fresh, seasonally available vegetables, but availability of durum wheat increased as the concept of large farms took hold and led to more widespread cultivation. This, combined with the development of a kneading machine and press, meant pasta could be produced in factories. If you visit the area, make time to visit the museum of pasta, the *Museo Storico Degli Spaghetti*, in Pontedassio, Italy.

I leave you now to ponder the wonders of pasta, its diversity and simple beauty. Now let's make pasta!

2 PASTA MAKING

HOW TO COOK AND STORE PASTA

Before we begin cooking pasta, I want to explain to you the way this most wonderful dish is served in Italy. The pasta is normally eaten as part of a four-plus-course meal, served after the antipasti starter and so normally known as *primi*. The portions are generally a little smaller than we are used to, normally around 70g of pasta per person. As a main dish you are looking to cook around 100g per person. This is only a guide. Appetite and how much pasta I alone can consume normally plays a large part in the amount I suggest, so please do not be too strict; these are only guidelines.

Pasta is so easy to cook correctly and yet it can very easily go terribly wrong. There are a few essential rules that you need to follow in order to ensure the perfect al *dente bite* every time:

1 Choose the type of pasta according to the sauce and dish you will be making. I adore penne, or *rigatoni rigate*, which has a furrowed ridge that runs along or around the body of the pasta. This type tends to absorb the sauce more easily. Penne that is smooth is known as *lisce*.
2 Every type of pasta has a different cooking time. Timings can differ from the brand of pasta to whether or not you are cooking dried pasta or fresh egg pasta; egg pasta cooks much quicker.
3 Dried pasta in packets. I recommend you follow the cooking instructions but stop cooking 2 minutes before the time given on the packet. This will leave you with an *al dente* bite every time. Remember, sometimes the pasta is also returned to a stove top pan after draining to combine with a sauce, so this will give it additional cooking time.
4 Portion size is something that most people, especially Italian pasta lovers, struggle with. I always seem to cook far too much, but if I'm honest this isn't a problem in my house as I love leftover pasta. The average standard portion size, as I said above, is 100g uncooked per person unless you are my mum, in which case this will easily be doubled.
5 Before we go any further I think we need to dispel the myth of it being helpful to add oil to pasta water while cooking. Oil is NOT required. It will not stop pasta from sticking. The oil will simply sit on top of the water (as oil and water do not mix), and to be honest I think of it as a waste of oil. I only use a little oil in pasta water when I make *pastina* or minestrone soup. However, drizzle away a good quality extra virgin olive oil to finish your plated-up dish; this will add flavour.

To cook

1 Fill a large wide saucepan with water and bring to a boil.

2 Once the water has started to boil (rolling boil), salt it well. Do not salt the water any sooner as it will take longer to come to a boil. Per 100g of pasta you will need 1 litre of water and 10g of salt. Please note the pasta will only draw the required amount of salt needed.

3 Add the pasta to the pan and stir well with a wooden spoon. No oil is required in the pasta water unless you are making a minestrone soup.

4 Cook the pasta for the recommended time and taste. There should be a little resistance when you bite into the pasta (*al dente*). Drain and continue with preparing your dish.

How to store fresh pasta

I would say that the stage of storing fresh pasta is almost as important as making the pasta thinly and in the correct manner, as well as cooking it correctly using sufficient water and the correct amount of salt.

1 A freshly made ball of dough will keep well in the fridge for 36–48 hours, wrapped in cling film.

2 Any short, unfilled pasta can be left on trays or tea towels that have been dusted with polenta or semolina. The pasta must be turned daily. After four to five days and once completely dry, the pasta can be stored in an airtight container for up to nine months. Once dried, this type of pasta can be frozen (see point 4).

3 Long fresh pasta can be made and left to dry on wooden poles, racks or hangers. The pasta can also be rolled into loosely formed bird's nests. The nests would need to be turned twice a day in order to allow plenty of air to circulate around the pasta as it dries. Allow seven days for the nests to dry fully and then store in airtight containers. This type of pasta can also be frozen once dried (see point 4).

4 Filled pasta, such as tortellini and ravioli, can also be frozen for convenience. The prepared pasta should be allowed to air-dry for at least an hour. Then it can be laid out on baking trays in single layers and placed into the freezer for 2 hours. Once the filled pasta has frozen, tumble each piece carefully into freezer bags and store for up to 3 months. Cooking the pasta from frozen will take an additional 2–3 minutes.

HOW TO MAKE PASTA BY HAND

Making a Simple Egg Pasta Dough

Sfogline are ladies who specialise in rolling freshly made pasta dough into *una sfoglia*, a huge see-through sheet of pasta. Here is a quote I recently heard and wanted to share with you: '*Sfogline* are known to say that the pasta dough is ready when you hear it sing.' To sing means you hear and also feel bubbles popping as you knead the dough with the heels of your hands.

So many people are afraid of making fresh handmade pasta, but I don't understand why. I agree that ready-made dried pasta is affordable and a great staple store-cupboard ingredient (I have more than twenty dried packets in my larder at any one time). However, a bowl of freshly handmade pasta is simply mouth-watering from the first to the very last bite. In my opinion, fresh pasta is superior to dried pasta not only in taste but also in texture and colour. When making fresh egg pasta, '00' soft wheat flour is used; this type has been milled to a superfine powder and is much finer than other flours.

There are many different flours and flour blends that make wonderful pasta. From a nutty farro spelt flour to chestnut flour, rye flour, buckwheat flour, kamut flour and many more, as well as the much-loved '0' flour and semolina flour. They each work well individually but also when blended with a '00' soft wheat flour.

There are a couple of general guidelines that are useful when making fresh egg pasta dough

▶ 100g '00' flour plus 1 large egg equals one portion of pasta dough. This can vary and be adjusted with different flour blends.

▶ For a richer dough you can use just egg yolks and omit the whites (save the whites to make a meringue or egg white omelette).

▶ 400g '00' flour plus 12 egg yolks makes a rich pasta dough that is perfect for ravioli etc.

EGG PASTA DOUGH

PASTA FRESCA FATTO A MANO

Preparation time 1 hour
(including resting)
Serves 4

––––––––

400g '00' flour
4 large eggs
Pinch of salt (optional)

1 Ideally, work on a wooden or marble board but a wooden tabletop would work well too. I prefer to use a wooden surface as this gives a little added texture to the dough and helps in the kneading process. Tip the flour onto the board and form a well in the centre with your fingers (I call this a volcano).

2 Crack the eggs into the well (volcano) and add a pinch of salt. The salt is optional and if I'm honest, I generally eliminate the salt from my fresh pasta as I tend to salt the pasta water well instead.

3 With your fingertips or a fork gently introduce the flour to the egg mixture, being careful to not break the walls of the volcano and lose any of the egg mixture.

4 Form the mixture into a pliable dough. If there is any excess flour that will not incorporate into the dough, scrape it away.

5 Knead the dough using the heels of both hands until the dough has become smooth and silky with a light spring back when pushed with your fingertip. Kneading by hand will take around 7–10 minutes.

6 If the dough is a little dry, add 1–2 tablespoons of water or milk; if it is too wet add a little more flour. Just remember that adding too much flour can lead to a dry and slightly denser dough.

7 Wrap the dough with cling film and allow to rest for a minimum of 30 minutes at room temperature.

8 Once the dough has rested, you can either work or roll the dough by hand using a very thin rolling pin (I use a wooden broom handle), or alternatively a pasta machine. Using a pasta machine allows the dough to become silky and guarantees a smooth finish.

9 However much dough you make, you must always work with it in portions when using a pasta machine. Cut the dough in half. Take the first half and wrap the remaining half in cling film to ensure the dough does not dry out and form an outer skin.

10 Set the pasta machine to the widest setting. Each machine will differ so please follow your manufacturer's instructions as required.

11 Flatten and lightly flour the dough then feed it through the pasta machine. Fold the dough back over itself (like an envelope) and feed through the widest setting again at least six times. This will ensure smoothness and elasticity.

12 Increase a notch at a time on the machine and feed the dough through on each setting twice. There is no need to envelope the dough at this stage; you are just trying to lengthen it.

13 Continue rolling the dough, narrowing the rollers at every stage.

14 I tend to stop at the second to last thinnest section on the pasta machine. This is the appropriate thickness required for perfect pasta; you should be able to read a newspaper through the pasta sheet.

15 As an alternative option I also press herbs into my pasta at this stage, so if you are feeling creative have a go. Take the pasta sheet and cover half of the sheet with parsley leaves, tiny basil leaves or baby thyme or oregano leaves. Small edible flowers could also be used. Please note the leaves must be soft and stem-free otherwise the dough will rip.

16 Fold the plain pasta half over the herb-covered dough and push down gently using the palm of your hand, to secure. Press through the pasta machine one last time. You should be left with a sheet of beautifully decorated pasta.

17 The pasta sheet once rolled should be approximately 3mm in thickness.

18 Now choose your shape – from spaghetti, linguine, lasagne sheets, tagliatelle or a perfect base for a filled ravioli, mezzaluna, tortellini or anolini.

LA SFOGLIA
(HAND-ROLLED PASTA SHEET)

Of course you have the choice and ease of using a pasta machine nowadays, either a hand-cranked one that has pride of place on your kitchen surface or a modern electric machine with a specialist attachment. However, my Nonna Carmela at eighty-seven years old still only rolls her pasta with a rolling pin or broom handle to obtain her perfect pasta *sfoglia*. This is the traditional method used and preferred by the older generation. Rolling with a pin is a great technique to master and requires a little skill and copious amounts of elbow grease.

Preparation time 15 minutes plus 30 minutes resting
Serves 4

400g '00' flour
4 large eggs

———

1 Make and knead the dough as for the egg pasta on page 13.

2 Wrap and allow the dough to rest for a minimum of 30 minutes.

3 There's no need to halve the dough into portions when using this rolling pin method. Push the ball of dough into a large flat disc with your hands.

4 Place the rolling pin in the centre of the pasta dough and begin to roll as you would a sheet of pastry.

5 Roll the dough; do not fold it. Ensure you flour the sheet as required to prevent sticking. As the sheet becomes larger, gently hang it over the edge of the table and continue to roll. Hanging the sheet over the edge of the table will aid in stretching the dough.

6 Turn the dough through 90 degrees and continue to roll it until you have reached the perfect smooth *sfoglia* sheet.

7 The thickness of the *sfoglia* will really depend on the shape you intend to make. I always aim to make my sheet almost see-through – approximately 3–4mm thick.

MAKING PASTA FOR FILLING

What's your favourite filling? What's your favourite filled pasta shape? They each have their own identity along with their unique shape and perfect form. Each filled pasta shape has its place in a certain region of Italy, a sense of belonging. In essence they are very similar to each other; it may only be folding or pinching in a certain way that differentiates them from each other.

Filling ideas are included within the recipe section of the book, but I have to say I have a love for the classic blend of ricotta, nutmeg, wilted spinach and Parmesan (page 86). Tortellini in *brodo* (broth or stock) was always my medicinal cure when I was growing up. If I felt poorly or a little under the weather then pasta in *brodo* would soon have me fighting fit. Ravioli and agnolotti remind me of special family occasions and celebrations. Nowadays I make them weekly for my own family, so there's no need for it to be a special occasion at *Casa Sereno* to enjoy filled pasta, or any type of pasta to be honest. Every day is a celebration.

CONVERSIONS

IMPERIAL	METRIC	AMERICAN
½ fl oz	15 ml	1 tablespoon
1 fl oz	30 ml	⅛ cup
2 fl oz	60 ml	¼ cup
4 fl oz	120 ml	½ cup
8 fl oz	240 ml	1 cup
16 fl oz	480 ml	1 pint
4oz	100g	
7oz	200g	
10oz	300g	
13oz	400g	
1lb	500g	

In British, Australian and often Canadian recipes an imperial pint is 20 fl oz. American recipes use the American pint measurement, which is 16 fl oz.

TORTELLINI

Tiny tortellini remind me of delicate little belly buttons. They're beautifully formed and delicious in either *brodo* (broth), browned butter and sage, or a simple seasonal tomato and basil sauce.

———————

1 Cut the prepared pasta dough in half, wrap one half in cling film or a clean tea towel and roll out the remaining dough using either a pasta machine, rolling pin or broom handle to a thickness of 3mm. Repeat with the remaining dough. I prefer to use my pasta machine to press the pasta into two large lasagne sheets, approximately 15–20cm in length.
2 Cut the pasta sheets into either squares 4cm x 4cm or small circles 5cm in diameter.
3 Add a teaspoon of filling to the centre of each pasta shape.
4 Take the pasta in both hands and fold the pasta squares in half to form triangles or the circles in half as if making a *mezzaluna* (half moon).
5 Pinch the pasta dough around the filling, removing any excess air as required.
6 Pointing the triangle up towards the ceiling (or if you have made circles, the curve to the ceiling), take each corner and bring them together, one in front of the other, to create a tortellini shape.

Preparation time 1 hour using ready-made dough
Serves 4

———————

400g fresh egg pasta dough (page 13)
Filling of choice

RAVIOLI

These popular filled pasta parcels are easy to make. Just choose your favourite shape — from a simple square to a triangle or circle.

1 Cut the prepared pasta dough in half, wrap one half in cling film or a clean tea towel and roll out the remaining dough with either a pasta machine, rolling pin or broom handle to the thickness of 3mm. I prefer to use my pasta machine as I gain a silky pasta finish. Press the pasta into two large lasagne sheets approximately 15cm wide.

2 Take one sheet and place individual teaspoonfuls of filling across the length of one piece of dough, leaving an approximate gap of 4cm between each mound.

3 Dip your finger in a little water and lightly dampen around the filling.

4 Place the top layer of pasta directly over the base sheet.

5 Gently use your hands to cup the filling between the pasta layers, removing and pushing out any excess air.

6 Seal the pasta by pinching around each and use a knife, pastry cutter, or shaped cutter if you prefer, to cut the ravioli into shapes.

7 Lay the ravioli on a tray that has been lightly dusted with polenta and use the remaining pasta in the same way to make more.

Preparation time 1 hour using ready-made dough
Serves 4

400g fresh egg pasta dough (page 13)
Filling of choice

FRESH EGG YOLK RAVIOLO

This pasta dish is different and a little unusual. It is basically a large filled pasta circle with a fresh egg yolk nestled into the filling. Rich and totally worth the effort, it is simple to master so please give it a go at your next dinner party. The aim once prepared is to cook it for a specific length of time to ensure a dippy egg yolk centre.

Preparation time 1 hour using
ready-made dough
Serves 4

400g fresh egg pasta dough (page 13)
Filling of choice
8 large egg yolks
Rock salt

1 Make and roll your dough as for the ravioli recipe (page 18) and roll it into long sheets using your pasta machine or rolling pin. Use a 10cm round cutter to cut out multiple discs of dough as required. One raviolo would make a perfect starter or serve two per person as a main course.

2 Pipe the filling (I like to use a classic spinach and ricotta) onto one disc in a circle, leaving a 1cm gap around the edge and ensuring there is enough room in the centre of the filling to drop in an egg yolk.

3 Drop a fresh egg yolk into the centre of the filling and add a tiny pinch of coarse rock salt to the top of the yolk.

4 To help the top layer of pasta stick to the bottom, lightly wet your finger in a little water and dampen the edge of the base pasta disc.

5 Place a disc of pasta on top and press it down at one side. Gently pull the top disc and continue to attach it to the base by pushing down all the way round, trying to eliminate any air. Ensure the raviolo is pinched all the way around.

6 Use the remaining pasta to make more in the same way.

7 Cook in salted boiling water for 2 minutes 40 seconds – this will ensure you are left with a dippy egg yolk – then serve with melted butter and sage.

DOUBLE RAVIOLI
DOPPIO RAVIOLI

Having the beauty of a ravioli but with two deliciously matched flavoured fillings, this pasta will take a little patience to master but it's worth persevering – the result is delicious. What two fillings would you choose to complement each other? Maybe a smooth mushroom filling paired with a ricotta, or a roasted pepper and butternut squash combination. The choices are endless.

Preparation time 1 hour 15 minutes using ready-made dough
Serves 4

400g fresh egg pasta dough (page 13)
2 fillings of choice

1 Make, prepare and roll your pasta dough into long sheets as for the ravioli recipe (page 18).
2 Prepare two fillings that would complement each other – for example, one could be a ricotta filling and one a mixed mushroom and thyme – and transfer them to disposable piping bags.
3 Cut the pasta into long sheets, 10cm wide by 60cm long.
4 Pipe one type of filling along the length of the dough on one side, 2cm from the edge.
5 Leave a 1cm gap and pipe the other flavoured filling alongside the first filling.
6 Fold the dough over to cover the fillings. Using a plastic pastry scraper apply pressure in between the fillings, encouraging the pasta to sit proud over each filling. Press the dough down along the long edge, removing any excess air.
7 Pinch the dough that includes the fillings at 4cm intervals all the way along, top and bottom.
8 Take a pastry roller and cut the dough along the pinched sections of dough. This will leave you with a double ravioli. Repeat as required. It's fiddly but fantastic!

ANOLINI

Anolini are in essence ravioli but without the pasta skirt surround. You will need a small circular cutter to make these little pillows. It really is in essence a pasta dumpling – perfect if you are in the mood for filled pasta but would prefer a lighter option.

1 Cut the prepared pasta dough in half, wrap one half in cling film and

Preparation time 1 hour using
ready-made dough
Serves 4

400g fresh egg pasta dough (page 13)
Filling of choice

begin rolling the remainder. Roll the pasta out into long lasagne sheets using a pasta machine (page 13).

2 Take one sheet and place small teaspoonfuls of filling across the length of the dough, leaving a gap of approximately 4cm between each spoonful.

3 Dip your finger in a little water and lightly dampen around the filling. Place the top layer of pasta directly over the base sheet.

4 Slowly and carefully use your hands to cup the pasta and filling, removing any excess air from the pockets.

5 Seal the pasta, pressing down with your fingertips securely, and use the anolini cutter to press down around each pasta mound. You will be left with tiny pasta dumplings, minus a pasta skirt.

6 Lay the anolini on a tray that has been lightly dusted with polenta and use the remaining pasta in the same way to make more.

AGNOLOTTI

These are ravioli from the Piedmonte region of Italy, where they are simply known by a different name. The only difference is the way they are connected together and pinched.

Preparation time 1 hour using
ready-made dough
Serves 4

400g fresh egg pasta dough (page 13)
Fillling of choice

1 Cut the prepared pasta dough in half, wrap one half in cling film or a clean tea towel and roll the remaining pasta out using either a pasta machine, rolling pin or broom handle to the thickness of a 5p piece. I prefer to use my pasta machine and press the pasta into two large lasagne sheets (page 13).

2 Take one sheet and place teaspoonfuls of filling across the length of dough, leaving a gap of approximately 4cm between each spoonful.

3 Dip your finger in a little water and lightly dampen around the filling.

4 Place the top layer of pasta directly over the base sheet and filling.

5 Slowly use your hands to secure the pasta dough around the filling. Pinch the dough in between each *agnolotto* so that they are all attached.

6 Use a pastry cutter or sharp knife and cut across each attached piece of dough to separate the *agnolotti*.

7 Lay the *agnolotti* on a tray that has been lightly dusted with polenta and use the remaining pasta in the same way to make more.

MAKING UNFILLED PASTA SHAPES

Making pasta by hand is a pleasure, especially if you have your children or grandchildren around the kitchen table to help. Pasta making can become part of your family tradition, whether it's a simple egg dough for leggy spaghetti or a slightly more complex handmade *sorprese* or *garganelli*.

I remember as a child being in Nonna Carmela's small spare bedroom and seeing the large cotton checked tablecloth she had laid on the bed and covered with delicately hand-rolled pasta – beautifully crafted *orecchiette*, *fusilli* and my favourite, *cicatelli*. Such wonderful memories of growing up with pasta are the ones I would like to instil in my children: the sense of preparing, cooking and eating as a family. I had to include a few photos of another favourite shape known as little hats or 'Cappelli'. My children love making these as well as eating them. They are incredibly simple and fun to make. Take a disc of pasta and halve it then form the half into a cone shape and secure by pinching it with your fingers. Place the cone, point size down (just the tip), into a glass bottle and push down with the palm of your hand; be sure to use a little force. The *cappelli* make the perfect pasta vessel to carry a meat based sauce.

Over the page I have listed some of my favourite hand-rolled shapes for you to try.

CORZETTI PASTA DOUGH

Corzetti pasta is a circular pressed flat pasta shape from the Liguria region. Wooden stamps are used to obtain the decorative design; many years ago each family had a wooden press with their coat of arms embedded in the disc. I have become a collector of pasta tools, which I'm sure is of no surprise at all. The stamps can now be purchased online from the stockist I recommend at the end of the book (page 244). *Corzetti* work incredibly well with a simple drizzle of pesto, tomato sauce or a heavier veal sugo (sauce).

Preparation time 45 minutes using ready-made dough
Serves 4

1 large egg (60g in weight)
120ml white wine or vermouth
360g '00' flour

1 Whisk the whole egg and wine together.
2 Tip the flour onto a wooden board (or into a bowl) and make a well in the centre.
3 Add the wet ingredients gently.
4 Slowly begin to combine the wet mixture with the flour, either using your fingers or a fork.
5 Form into a ball and work the dough for 5 minutes until smooth. Wrap in cling film and set aside for 30 minutes to rest at room temperature.
6 Roll the *corzetti* dough out with a large thin rolling pin to the thickness of a lasagne sheet.
7 Flour the *corzetti* stamp (top and bottom) to stop the pasta from sticking.
8 Cut out discs with the stamp cutter and then place each pre-cut disc onto the opposite side of the cutter.
9 Take the stamp, push down and press. This will imprint a design. Repeat with the remaining *corzetti* discs, allow to dry for 20 minutes and cook as required.

MALLOREDDUS
GNOCCHETTI SARDI

Beautiful *malloreddus* or *gnocchi sardi* from Sardinia are small, shell-like shapes made from a simple dough of hot water and semolina flour. Nuggets of dough are rolled with your thumb to form small ridges. I use a gnocchi board to make them (gnocchi boards are available online), but my nonna would always use a cheese grater, rolling the dough down the fine grater. They're simply scrumptious with sausages and tomatoes, a dish known as *gnocchi alla campidanese*.

Preparation time: 1 hour 15 minutes (depending how quickly your thumbs work)
Serves 4

400g semolina flour
(*semola di grano duro rimacinata*)
200ml hot water

1 Tip the flour onto a wooden board (or into a bowl) and make a well in the centre.
2 Pour half the hot water into the well and begin to work the flour in, then add the remaining water as required.
3 Form a ball of dough and knead for 5 minutes until smooth and elastic.
4 Cover and set aside. Allow to rest for a minimum of 30 minutes.
5 Flour your gnocchi board.
6 Pinch out a blueberry-sized piece of dough and roll it into a ball.
7 Place the dough at the top of the gnocchi board and use your thumb to push the dough down. This should create a shell shape with a slight indent in the centre. Continue in the same way with the remaining dough.

STROZZAPRETTI

I was taught to make *strozzapretti* on a recent trip to Romagna by a lovely lady known as Nonna Violante, my newly adopted nonna. The technique is simple to master but a little time consuming.

———

1 Prepare the dough in the same way as the egg pasta dough (page 13).

2 Allow the dough to rest for 30 minutes.

3 Halve the dough and work with one section at a time to make it easier to roll out. Cover one half with cling film and set aside.

4 Roll out the pasta dough either with a thin rolling pin to the thickness of a lasagne sheet or use a pasta machine and follow the instructions on page 13.

5 I use the tagliatelle attachment on the pasta machine, cutting the lasagne sheet into ribbons.

6 Take a tagliatelle and hold it in between your palms.

7 Slide your palms one way and the other; this will twist a short length of the pasta strip.

8 Once twisted, pinch the *strozzapretti* to detach it from the tagliatelle strip and continue with the remaining strands.

Preparation time 1 hour when using ready-made dough
Serves 4

———

400g '00' flour
4 large eggs

SORPRESE

Sorprese are also referred to as an unfilled tortellini and resemble tiny belly buttons. I adore this shape purely for its simplicity, but also for the fact that I still believe it is a relatively unknown shape.

————

1 Tip the flour onto a wooden board (or into a bowl) and make a well in the centre.
2 Crack the eggs into the centre of the well and begin to incorporate gently using either a fork or your fingertips.
3 Form into a dough and knead for 5 minutes until smooth and elastic.
4 Cover the dough and allow to rest for a minimum of 30 minutes.
5 Work in sections. Halve the dough and roll one half of the dough out with either a rolling pin or through a pasta machine as explained on page 13.
6 Roll the dough out into large lasagne sheets and cut into small 4cm x 4cm squares.
7 Take a square and make a triangle by pinching the top points together.
8 Then take the other two corners, fold them the other way and pinch them together.
9 Repeat with the remaining squares.

Preparation time 1 hour 30 minutes
Serves 4

————

400g '00' flour
4 large eggs

LORIGHITTAS

From the region of Sardinia, these delicate pasta ropes take a little skill to master but only a few minutes to enjoy a complete bowlful.

————

1 Tip the flour onto a board and make a well in the centre.

2 Add the water and combine. Form into a ball of dough and knead for 5 minutes.

3 Cover and allow to rest for 30 minutes.

4 Cut the dough into 8 portions. Roll each portion out into long thin sausages, 1.5mm in diameter by 23cm long – the thickness of a *pici* pasta or just a little thinner.

5 Take the long pasta and double loop the dough around three fingers so that you have two pasta bracelets. Pinch the dough to break off the remaining length of dough leaving you with only the two loops.

6 Twist the bracelets into each other to create a rope effect. Place on a tray that has been lightly dusted with polenta. Continue with the remaining dough.

Preparation time 1 hour 30 minutes
Serves 4

————

400g semolina flour
(*semola di grano duro*)
200ml hot water

ORECCHIETTE

When I think of *orecchiette* I think of the streets of Bari in Puglia but also of Nonna Carmela. Only recently I was lucky enough to make *orecchiette* again with her. She was fast and for every ten she made I managed an embarrassing two. In Bari all of the passion from the busy kitchens spills onto the steps and streets of this port city in what is a truly communal activity – the preparation of *orecchiette*, also known as 'little ears'.

Preparation time 1 hour 30 minutes
Serves 4

400g semolina flour
(*semola di grano duro*)
200ml hot water

1 Prepare the dough as for the *lorighittas* (page 27) and allow to rest for a minimum of 30 minutes.
2 Portion the dough into four equal amounts and roll each section into long sausages, the thickness of your little finger.
3 Cut each sausage into acorn amounts of dough.
4 Take a knife (I use a large blunt-edged butter knife), place it on top of an acorn of dough and drag the knife towards you. This will stretch the pasta.
5 Form the dough by pulling it over your thumb. This will leave you with small caps or tiny ears. Repeat with the remaining pasta.
6 Alternatively, take an acorn of dough and push down firmly with your thumb; this method is perfect for children to master.

CICATELLI OR CAVATELLI

Known as *cicatelli* in Puglia and *cavatelli* in Molise, when I think of *cicatelli* pasta I think of the goodie bags I'd receive from Nonna Carmela periodically throughout the year: bags full of handmade dried pasta. Now, due to her age, these goodie bags arrive less frequently; however, she has passed the skill of making *cicatelli* on to me, her eldest grandchild. Now I can return the favour.

———

Preparation time 1 hour using ready-made dough
Serves 4

———

400g semolina flour
(*semola di grano duro*)
200ml hot water

1 Prepare the dough as for the *lorighittas* (page 27) and allow to rest for a minimum of 30 minutes.
2 Portion the dough into four equal amounts and roll each section into long sausages, the thickness of your little finger.
3 Cut each sausage into 3cm pieces.
4 Take a piece of pasta and use your index and middle finger to indent the dough. Repeat with the remaining dough.
5 You can also, if preferred, purchase a *cavatelli* maker, which is incredibly fast and easy to use. If you intend to make them often and love the shape then this would be a very good investment.

FUSILLI, BUSIATE, RICCI

A very beautiful yet relatively simple pasta shape to master, this pasta lends itself to many names. I bought a packet of fifty wooden BBQ skewers solely for making pasta and use these to twist the pasta strips around. You can also use a piece of spaghetti or a traditional *ferro*: a metal skewer that is used to help you twist pasta and which is traditionally passed down from generation to generation. Nonna Carmela's *ferro* is sixty years old. I call them fusilli and this is my foolproof method.

Preparation time 1 hour 30 minutes
Serves 4

—————

400g semolina flour
(*semola di grano duro*)
200ml hot water

1 Make and rest your dough as for the *lorighittas* (page 27).
2 Roll the rested pasta dough out with a rolling pin into a see-through sheet of dough.
3 Allow the dough to rest again for 10 minutes. Sprinkle with flour and roll the dough up into a loose sausage.
4 Using a sharp knife, cut ribbons of dough, the thickness of a tagliatelle.
5 Cut each tagliatelle into 10cm-length strips.
6 Take a wooden skewer or piece of spaghetti. Place the skewer on one corner of the tagliatelle and roll, creating a twisted fusilli.
7 Leave the rolled fusilli on the skewer for 10 minutes to dry while you repeat with another skewer.
8 Remove all skewers and allow the fusilli to dry for a further hour before cooking.
9 An alternative would to be to make *maccheroni al ferro* using the same dough. Roll the dough into thin sausages (the thickness of a lady's little finger).
10 Cut into 3cm pieces of pasta dough and place the *ferro* on top of the piece of dough. Apply pressure and roll back and forth with the palm of your hand until the shape is made and you have a *maccheroni* with a hole running through the centre.

COLOURING PASTA

As a child I remember pushing my tiny face up against the window of our local Italian deli on a Saturday morning and asking my mum Solidea to buy the coloured pasta that was sitting so beautifully in the window display for my sister and I. She would promptly say 'No' and buy an equally delicious yet plain brand instead. As an adult I still do the same, and by that I mean by looking at the pasta in awe and not pushing my face up against the deli window.

We have all visited Italy or nipped into our local Italian deli and picked up a bag of delicately striped pappardelle or simply designed *farfalle* or *garganelli*, usually as a gift. Our eyes are immediately drawn to the bright colours and I still feel a sense of amazement when I see them: 'How on earth do they make this coloured pasta?'

Colouring pasta has turned into a passion for me. It's an experimental passion though – so many colours and techniques work really well but then others fail very badly! It's about balance, the balance of dry and wet ingredients.

In this chapter I will show you how to make simple coloured pasta dough that you can then make into your preferred shape, and also a slightly more technical stripe, which is beautiful when rolled into *garganelli* (tubes) or pinched into *farfalle* (bows) or *sorprese*. I have included various recipes that use vegetables such as beetroot and peppers to colour the dough, as well as a spice and some more unusual ingredients.

Using vegetables

I never use synthetic colours, only vegetables and leaves, to colour my pasta. I have given recipes using (pre-cooked) beetroot, spinach and tomato, but of course there are many more you can try. Now I don't expect you to all start colouring pasta in your day-to-day busy lives; however, to have an understanding of the techniques is invaluable, great fun and a little addictive once mastered.

To make a standard egg-based pasta dough, the ratios are 100g '00' flour to 1 large egg (60g in weight). When colouring pasta the quantities of both dry and wet ingredients will vary greatly. For example, when making spinach pasta, the consistency of the dough will depend on how well you squeeze the water from the blanched spinach.

While it's true that spinach makes a very delicious green dough, blanched stinging nettles, asparagus, kale or basil and parsley would also work well. The list of vegetables or leaves you can use to colour pasta dough is endless, so do experiment and try something a little different. Roasted peppers are another favourite of mine. Either roast your own or use jarred peppers for convenience. Drain the peppers, dry them well with a kitchen towel and blitz for 30 seconds. Add the egg and blitz for a further 20 seconds until you have a smooth puree. Now make your pasta by tipping '00' flour onto a board, make a well or volcano and add the wet ingredients and continue as normal. That said, you can of course use vegetable powders to add colour instead. These are easier to work with for beginners.

Striping pasta adds an extra creative dimension to the whole colouring pasta experience. I always make a simple egg-based pasta dough as the base colour and then use an additional two or three colours to add stripes to the pasta sheet, as pictured below.

Recipe notes:

▶ In each recipe that follows you can also make the pasta dough in a food mixer. Simply add all ingredients and whizz together for one minute until a rough dough is formed, then tumble out and knead.

▶ No salt is added to any of my handmade pasta dough recipes (coloured or plain dough) as the pasta water and sauce will always be salted very well.

▶ Always cover the dough that you're not working with to save it from drying out.

▶ When striping your pasta dough you will need to work quickly to prevent the dough from drying out. Cover the dough that you are working with, while it's rolled out, with damp kitchen towels. When you are ready to work with the dough, simply discard the kitchen towels. You can now work at a slightly steadier pace.

▶ When using vegetables, coloured pasta doesn't necessarily take on their flavour. However, the black cuttlefish pasta (page 36) does retain the fishy aroma, so always bear this in mind when cooking your pasta.

▶ Once the dough has rested, halve it with a knife (covering the remaining half in cling film to prevent it drying out) as this will make it much easier to work with. Roll the dough with either a pasta machine, rolling pin or wooden broom handle and then make your chosen shape.

SPINACH PASTA DOUGH

Preparation time 45 minutes
(including resting)
Serves 2

―――――

100g fresh spinach (blanched weight 50g)
1 large egg
200g '00' flour

1 Blanch the dry spinach in a dry frying pan on a low heat for 2 minutes until the spinach is fully wilted. Remove from the heat.

2 Squeeze excess water from the spinach with your hands, then enclose the spinach in a clean tea towel and squeeze tightly again. Do this a few times, making sure you wring it well. Spinach holds a lot of water, so you need to ensure as much of it is removed as possible otherwise you will end up with a very wet pasta dough, and this of course will never do.

3 Put the spinach and egg into a food processor and blitz; alternatively, chop the spinach very finely and mix with the egg.

4 Tip the flour onto a wooden board or into a bowl if preferred.

5 Make a well or volcano in the centre of the flour and pour in the wet ingredients, be careful to not break the walls of flour.

6 Slowly incorporate the spinach and flour together to form a dough. Work from the inside out, using either your fingertips or a fork, if preferred. If the dough is a little wet, add an additional tablespoon of '00' flour.

7 Knead the spinach dough for 5 minutes until smooth and elastic. Cover and set aside for 30 minutes to rest.

TOMATO PASTA DOUGH

Preparation time 45 minutes
(including resting)
Serves 2

———

1 large egg
1 large egg yolk
60g tomato purée
200g '00' flour

1 Put the whole egg, egg yolk and tomato purée into a food processor. Blitz for 10 seconds.
2 Pour the flour onto a wooden board or into a bowl.
3 Make a well in the centre and add the wet ingredients.
4 Use a fork to slowly incorporate the flour from the inside out with the tomato mixture.
5 When you have a dough, knead well for 5 minutes until smooth and elastic. Cover and set aside for 30 minutes to rest.

BEETROOT PASTA DOUGH

Preparation time 45 minutes
(including resting)
Serves 2

———

1 large egg
75g beetroot, pre-cooked
200g '00' flour

1 Put the egg and beetroot into a food processor. Blitz for 30 seconds until the beetroot has incorporated fully with the egg.
2 Pour the flour onto a wooden board or into a bowl and make a well in the centre.
3 Add the deep purple beetroot mixture to the well and mix with a fork to incorporate slowly, working with the flour from the inside out.
4 Form into a dough.
5 Knead for 5 minutes until smooth and elastic, cover and allow to rest for 30 minutes.

Using other ingredients

There are many other spices, herbs and liquids that can be added to colour pasta. Experiment when it comes to spices and herbs. Two of my favourites are oregano and marjoram, but equally I love golden saffron strands running through the dough. Cocoa powder adds an indulgent scrumptious colour and flavour. Pig's blood, red wine and cuttlefish ink anyone? You are probably thinking, no way! All I will say is that the cuttlefish ink adds a fabulous deep sea colour and pig's blood adds a certain depth.

SAFFRON PASTA DOUGH

Preparation time 45 minutes
(including resting)
Serves 2

2 large eggs
Pinch of saffron
200g '00' flour

1 Crack the eggs into a bowl and add the delicate saffron strands, whisk well and set aside. Alternatively, if preferred, crack the eggs straight into the prepared flour volcano with the saffron strands

2 Tip the flour onto a wooden board or into a bowl if preferred.

3 Make a well in the centre and pour in the eggs.

4 Incorporate the eggs into the flour gently, ensuring the walls of the well remain intact. The saffron will add a light amber colour to the dough with a delicious hit of punchy flavour.

5 Using a fork or your index finger work the egg mixture with the flour until you are able to form the flour into a dough.

6 Work into a dough, knead the dough for 5 minutes until smooth and elastic. Cover and set aside for 30 minutes.

CUTTLEFISH/SQUID INK PASTA DOUGH

Preparation time 45 minutes
(including resting)
Serves 2

———

2 large eggs
14g cuttlefish ink
200g '00' flour

1 Crack the eggs into a bowl and squeeze in the cuttlefish ink.
Using a fork, whisk together.
2 Tip the flour onto a wooden board or into a bowl if preferred.
Make a well in the centre of the flour.
3 Pour the fragrant black mixture into the well.
4 Using a fork, work the squid ink into the flour. Form a dough
(your hands will be black and fragrant).
5 Knead the dough for 5 minutes until smooth and elastic.
Cover and set aside for 30 minutes.

RED WINE PASTA DOUGH

Preparation time 1 hour
(including allowing red wine to
cool and dough to rest)
Serves 2

———

285ml red wine
1 large egg
200g '00' flour

1 Pour the red wine into a small saucepan. Reduce the wine down to
roughly half.
2 Allow the wine to cool fully.
3 Whisk the egg into the cold red wine.
4 Tip the flour onto a wooden board or into a bowl if preferred. Make a
well in the centre.
5 Pour the red wine and egg mixture into the well. Combine using a fork,
or fingertips if preferred, and form into a dough.
6 Knead for 5 minutes until smooth and elastic. Cover and set aside
for 30 minutes.

CHOCOLATE PASTA DOUGH

Preparation time 45 minutes
(including resting)
Serves 2
_____

2 large eggs
2 tbsps cocoa powder
200g '00' flour

1 Crack the eggs into a bowl, sieve the cocoa powder into the eggs and whisk with a fork.
2 Tip the flour onto a wooden board or into a bowl if preferred.
3 Pour the wet ingredients into the well. Use a fork to combine the eggs with the flour until you have a workable dough.
4 Knead the dough for 5 minutes until smooth and elastic. Cover and set aside for 30 minutes.

BLUTNUDELN
ITALIAN PASTA DOUGH USING PIG'S BLOOD (NOT VEGETARIAN FRIENDLY!)

Preparation time 45 minutes
(including resting)
Serves 2
_____

150g rye flour
150g '00' flour
1 large egg
120ml pig's blood (purchased from a good quality butchers)

I wanted to include this recipe in this section of the book for colouring techniques of course, but also more to bring awareness of the dish and the use of pig's blood. Please try to not be overly squeamish. The pasta does taste rich and with the rye flour, it is robust yet warming, almost autumnal. You can serve this pasta simply with melted butter, but I prefer it with a drizzle of peppery extra virgin olive oil. Play with the recipe. You can increase the number of eggs and reduce the volume of blood if you prefer. It's well worth having a go!

_____

1 Combine both flours together and tip them onto a wooden board.
2 Make a well in the centre of the flour.
3 Crack the egg into a small bowl and whisk together with the pig's blood.
4 Pour the mixture into the well of flour and use a fork to combine.
5 Use your hands to form the pasta into a ball of dough and knead it well for 5 minutes until soft and elastic. Wrap the dough in cling film and rest for 30 minutes before rolling.

HOW TO MAKE STRIPED PASTA DOUGH

Adding stripes to pasta is an art. This is one of my favourite pastimes; a sense of design takes over when I have coloured dough in my hand. However, I have recently changed my method. I used to hand-cut the coloured dough but discovered very quickly that I'm not very good with a knife and cut in an incredibly wonky fashion. Determination and patience is required. Let the creative side in you come out.

WHAT YOU NEED
Pasta machine (essential)
Small dough scraper knife

Small bowl of water
200g plain '00' fresh pasta dough
100g coloured dough of your choice,
e.g. beetroot

1 Start by making a plain '00' egg pasta dough (page 13). This will form the perfect surface for the base of your striped pasta.
2 Make your chosen coloured dough from the choice on pages 33–37. As before, cover and allow all the dough to rest fully before stretching.
3 Take the plain pasta dough and run it through the pasta machine as if making lasagne sheets (page 13). Try to not press the sheets any thinner than 4mm. Place the lasagne sheet on your work surface and cover with damp kitchen towels to prevent the dough from drying out.
4 Roll out the coloured pasta dough in the same way. Always flour the coloured dough well on both sides before rolling as in some instances this dough may hold a little more moisture than a standard plain pasta dough.
5 Run the coloured dough through the tagliatelle cutter on the pasta machine. Alternatively, allow the dough to dry for 20 minutes, flour it, 'envelope-fold' it and manually cut into tagliatelle.
6 Take the plain dough and trim off both raw edges.

7 Take a strand of the beetroot tagliatelle and dampen on one side with a little water. Place the strand damp side down onto the plain pasta. Continue in this way, leaving small gaps as desired to make stripes.

8 Once the sheet has been fully striped with the coloured tagliatelle, trim the raw edges.

9 Using your hand, gently apply pressure to the striped pasta to ensure the strands are fixed and in place.

10 Lightly flour the pasta on both sides.

11 Set the pasta machine to number 3 (a medium setting) and start rolling the sheet, once through on each setting until your desired thickness has been reached, approximately 3mm in thickness.

12 To alternate the coloured pasta stripes, simply use two or three different colours.

13 Cut and shape the pasta as required.

MAKING GLUTEN-FREE PASTA
PASTA SIN GLUTIN

Gluten has now become an issue with many pasta lovers in terms of the need to eliminate, change diet and find an alternative pasta that doesn't contain gluten. Gluten is what gives pasta or bread its structure and elasticity, so when we remove this structure we need to make sure that we provide a balance by using an alternative ingredient or two.

I am constantly asked about gluten-free pasta, with regards to a recipe or which brands are better than others. At my local Italian delicatessen, owner Adriana stocks gluten-free pasta made with quinoa flour, which makes a great and very delicious alternative. I have included three recipes for you to try. All I will say is persevere. The dough, due to there being no gluten, is rather brittle and can be a little stubborn to work with. You will need a pasta machine for the following method.

Preparation time 10 minutes, plus
30 minutes resting at room temperature
Serves 2 (multiply as required)

———————

STANDARD GLUTEN-FREE PASTA

160g rice flour
50g potato starch
2 tbsp xanthan gum
Pinch of salt
1 tbsp cornflour
1 tbsp olive oil
3 eggs

QUINOA GLUTEN-FREE PASTA

60g potato starch
80g quinoa flour
70g cornflour
1 tsp guar gum
2 tsp xanthan gum
Pinch of salt
2 whole eggs plus 4 yolks

BROWN RICE GLUTEN-FREE PASTA

190g brown rice flour
60g tapioca starch
1 tsp xanthan gum
Pinch of salt
4 eggs

———————

1 Choose your recipe and place all the ingredients into a food processor and blitz for one minute. I would always normally make my pasta by hand but find the food processor is the right choice for gluten-free.
2 Turn the dough out onto a wooden board and knead for 3–5 minutes until smooth.
3 Cover the dough in cling film or a clean tea towel and allow it to rest for 15–30 minutes.
4 Cut the dough in half, then wrap up one half and set aside.
5 Using a pasta machine, start at the widest setting. Take the dough and pat it down into a flat disc. Roll the dough through once then envelope or just fold (take the flattened dough and fold it in half) the dough and pass it through the widest setting four times. Gluten-free pasta will react differently and not be as firm as a traditional pasta dough, so please take your time.
6 Then change the setting to a slightly narrower setting and pass the dough through twice on each setting.
7 Work your way through to thinnest setting or until you have a pasta dough approximately 3mm thick.
8 Shape and cut your flat dough by using a knife to make *tagliatelle*, *farfalle* or whatever shape takes your fancy.
9 Cook the pasta until *al dente* or air-dry on racks and freeze.

3 RECIPES BY REGION

ABRUZZO

Abruzzo is located in central Italy bordering the regions of Molise, Umbria and Lazio. This picturesque region stretches from the Apennines to the warm Adriatic Sea, boasting beautiful L'Aquila as its capital. Snow-topped peaks encourage tourists to head out to the slopes for winter sports whilst no doubt enjoying the beautiful array of food that Abruzzo has to offer.

The region is so diverse and the recipes I have included in this chapter really have my taste buds in uproar, from the classic *spaghetti alla chitarra* to delicate *scrippelle* pancakes in stock and rich meat sauces with *maccheroni*. I would say this region still echoes the simplicity of cooking from the south of Italy, tailor-making dishes using seasonal produce from both inland and the warm coastline.

▲ Chillies, garlic and onions hang in the sun in Pescocostanzo, Abruzzo.

▶ Roccascalegna, a medieval castle in the mountains of Abruzzo.

ITALIAN CREPES ROLLED IN STOCK

SCRIPPELLE 'MBUSSE

This dish should really be served as a first course, but I just had to include it here as I often double the mixture and serve it as a main dish to my family. It's a light thin pancake dressed with chicken stock and a sprinkle of fresh herbs and pecorino. An alternative would be to fill the crepes with a spinach and ricotta filling, roll and lay in a baking dish topped with a sprinkle of pecorino before baking.

Preparation and chilling time 40 minutes
Cooking time 20 minutes
Serves 4

1l chicken or vegetable stock
260g '00' flour
6 large eggs
260ml milk
½ tsp grated nutmeg
2 tbsp pecorino
Small handful of parsley, finely chopped, plus extra to sprinkle
Salt and pepper to season
125g Parmesan, grated

1 Pour the stock into a saucepan and warm through gently.

2 Spoon the flour into a large mixing bowl.

3 Crack the eggs into another bowl and whisk.

4 Pour the milk into the eggs along with the grated nutmeg, 1 tablespoon of the pecorino, half the parsley, a pinch of salt and a twist of black pepper. Stir well to combine.

5 Slowly add the flour, whisking well so that no lumps form. The batter should be the consistency of double cream. Whisk well, cover and chill in the fridge for a minimum of 30 minutes.

6 Rub a 25cm crepe pan or frying pan with an oiled kitchen towel. Over a medium heat, add a small ladle of the batter, aiming for thin pancakes. Cook for 45 seconds on each side. Place on a plate then add a layer of baking parchment and continue to stack the crepes in this way. Drape a clean tea towel over the pancakes to keep them warm until all are completed. As a main dish, I would advise two or three pancakes each.

7 Sprinkle a little Parmesan over each pancake and roll each tightly.

8 Place three rolled pancakes into each bowl. Spoon over two ladles of stock. Sprinkle with additional Parmesan and parsley to serve.

CARMELA'S TIPS
Freeze excess pancakes once cooled for a quick lunch. Wrap in foil and store for up to 3 months.

HAND-ROLLED RIBBONS WITH A MIXED MEAT SAUCE

MACCHERONI ALLA MOLINARA

This pasta is incredible, to say the least. Completely different to anything I have ever made before. The meat from the sauce is removed and served as a second course. A steady pair of hands and short blunt nails will aid you. I find this a difficult pasta shape to explain but basically, imagine the shape of a fennel *tarallo* (small oval biscuits) then stretched into a long thin *tarallo*. Just remember that if the pasta loops break (mine always do) it's not the end of the world.

————

Preparation time 1 hour
Cooking time 3 hours
Serves 4

————

500g freshly prepared semolina dough
   (page 24)
Polenta, for dusting

FOR THE SAUCE
3 tbsp olive oil
1 carrot, peeled and cut into tiny cubes
1 celery stick, cut into tiny cubes
1 shallot, peeled and finely sliced
2 cloves garlic, peeled and finely sliced
300g rump steak, cut into
   4 equal portions
300g pork loin, cut into 4 equal portions
300g lamb steak, cut into
   4 equal portions
150g pancetta, cubed
3 x 400g tins plum tomatoes
1 tbsp tomato purée
1 small chilli (optional), deseeded
   and chopped
Pinch of dried oregano
Salt and pepper to season
Small bunch of basil, roughly torn
Parmesan rind (optional)
80g Parmesan, grated

1 Into a medium saucepan, add the olive oil along with the base for the *soffritto* (chopped vegetables), the carrot, celery and shallot. Cook gently over a medium heat for 10 minutes.

2 Add the garlic and stir.

3 Tumble in the rump steak, pork loin and lamb steak. Stir and sear all over.

4 Scatter over the pancetta and stir. Cook for a further 5 minutes.

5 Add the plum tomatoes, tomato purée, chilli and oregano and season with salt and pepper.

6 Add half the basil and stir. Cook over a low to medium heat for 3 hours. Check intermittently to stir and to alter seasoning if required.

7 I like to add a Parmesan rind into the sauce at this point as it adds great depth of flavour. This is, however, optional.

8 Take the prepared pasta dough and cut it in half. Cover one half with cling film and continue to work with the other.

9 Roll the dough into a ball and flatten it into a disc then use your index finger to make a hole in the centre.

10 Slowly work the dough with your fingers as you would a bagel or *tarallo* by making the centre hole larger. Stretch the dough's centre hole until it is large enough to fit both hands through it.

11 Keeping the dough in a ring start rolling the dough until it is a large hoop, a long once-piece skipping rope.

12 Roll the dough to the thickness of a piece of penne pasta and allow to dry for 10 minutes.

13 Take the pasta in one hand and coil it around so you have a collection of loops in your hand, each approximately 30cm in length.

14 Apply pressure and gently squeeze the dough to flatten the strands slightly. Moving the loop around your hard repeat this twice.

15 Lay the finished pasta on a light sprinkling of polenta.

16 Repeat with the other half of the dough.

17 Bring a large pan of water to a boil. Once boiling, salt well and add the coils of pasta. Cook until *al dente*.

18 Check the sauce and stir. Remove the meat from the sauce and place in a warmed serving dish.

19 Once the pasta is cooked, drain, reserving a ladle of starchy pasta water.

20 Tumble the pasta into the sauce along with the reserved pasta water and stir. Scatter over 30g of Parmesan and combine.

21 Serve the pasta in a large warm serving dish. Sprinkle over the remaining basil and Parmesan.

22 Serve the meat in the centre of the table with a salad for the second course. *Buono!*

CHITARRA PASTA WITH RAGU
MACCHERONI ALLA CHITARRA CON RAGU

I remember when I first became aware of a *chitarra*, a wooden rectangular frame with strings. The fact that it is a regional pasta tool fills me with happiness as I'm a collector of traditional pasta-making tools. My children call it our kitchen guitar but I always refer to it as my pasta harp. The *chitarra* can be easily purchased online; alternatively cut the pasta by hand into 3mm strips. When I think of Abruzzo, it automatically conjures up images of thin sheets of freshly made pasta laid delicately and rolled over the fine strings, leaving you with beautiful even strands of long flat spaghetti, ready to be coated in your chosen sauce.

————

1 Take the ready-made pasta dough and cut it in half, covering one portion with cling film or a clean tea towel so that it doesn't dry out.
2 Using either a rolling pin or pasta machine, roll out the dough into thin lasagne sheets 20cm wide by 40cm in length.
3 Lay a pasta sheet onto the *chitarra* and use a rolling pin to apply pressure, rolling the pin back and forth until the pasta falls through the strings.
4 Continue in the same way with the remaining dough and lie all the strands on a tray or clean tea towel dusted with polenta.
5 Into a sauté pan, add the olive oil and gently fry off the garlic over a medium heat for 3 minutes.
6 Add the carrot and celery, fry off gently over a medium heat for 7 minutes.
7 Tumble in the small pieces of lamb and colour all over; this will take about 10 minutes.
8 Pour in the plum tomatoes and add the chilli. Use the back of a wooden spoon to break up the tomatoes.
9 Squeeze in the tomato purée, season with salt and pepper and stir.
10 Scatter in the celery leaves, half the parsley and basil. Stir and leave to simmer for 1 hour 30 minutes until the lamb is tender.
11 Place a large pan of water on to boil. Once boiling, salt well and add the pasta.
12 Cook the pasta until *al dente* (with a bite). Drain, reserving a small ladle of pasta water.
13 Toss the pasta into the sauce and stir. Add the remaining herbs and half the Parmesan. Stir and serve in warm bowls with a sprinkle of Parmesan.

Preparation time 1 hour
Cooking time 30 minutes
Serves 4

————

400g prepared pasta dough
    (page 13)
Polenta, for dusting
2 tbsp olive oil
2 garlic cloves, peeled and crushed
1 carrot, peeled and finely cubed
1 celery stick, finely cubed
400g lamb, sinew removed, cut into
    small cubes
2 x 400g tins plum tomatoes
1 small red chilli, deseeded and
    finely sliced
1 tbsp tomato purée
Salt and pepper to season
Small handful of celery leaves,
    finely sliced
Small bunch of parsley, finely chopped
15 basil leaves, roughly torn
100g Parmesan, grated

CARMELA'S TIPS
You could substitute the fresh pasta with ready-made linguine or spaghetti.

————

SIMPLE CHEESE AND EGG PASTA

PASTA CACIO E OVA

With this recipe I give you a speedy lunch or supper ready in less than 15 minutes. A classic from Abruzzo, with minimum ingredients, this recipe echoes the influence of *cucina povera* cooking. It's a great dish as it is but equally, you can add in peas with the pasta and pancetta with the garlic to add more flavour, colour and texture. A basic take on a carbonara, when made well it's an absolute winner.

———

Preparation time 5 minutes
Cooking time 15 minutes
Serves 4

———

400g pasta tubes
3 tbsp olive oil
1 large clove garlic, peeled
4 large eggs
80g Parmesan, grated (plus extra to sprinkle)
Salt and pepper to season
Small handful of celery leaves, finely chopped
Small bunch of parsley, finely chopped

1 Place a large pan of water on to boil. Once boiling, salt well and add the pasta. Cook the pasta tubes until *al dente*.
2 Pour the oil into a shallow pan and add the garlic clove. Allow the oil to warm through absorbing the flavours of the garlic clove. After 5 minutes remove the oil from the heat and discard the garlic clove.
3 Crack the eggs into a large bowl and whisk.
4 Add the Parmesan along with a pinch of salt and good twist of black pepper and stir.
5 Scatter in the celery leaves and half the parsley and combine.
6 Drain the pasta, reserving a small ladle of starchy pasta water.
7 Tumble the pasta into the aromatic oil and stir.
8 Pour in the eggy mixture and stir well. If required, add a little pasta water to loosen up the pasta; this will also help to emulsify the sauce.
9 Scatter through the remaining parsley and serve in warm bowls with an additional sprinkle of Parmesan.

CARMELA'S TIPS
For an even quicker dish, you could use garlic-infused olive oil in step 2.

———

TRENNE PASTA WITH LEMON AND TUNA

TRENNE AL LIMONE E ATUNE

Imagine a large triangular penne pasta with ridges, and you have *trenne* pasta. It is a fabulous shape but as you can imagine possibly a little tricky to find in your local supermarket or deli. Penne makes a perfect alternative. This dish is zesty with a taste of the sea. Cheese isn't traditionally served with fish in Italy but I like to break the rules, adding a sprinkle of Parmesan with this dish, but this is optional.

———

Preparation time 10 minutes
Cooking time 25 minutes
Serves 4

———

400g trenne pasta (or penne)
2 tbsp olive oil
1 shallot, peeled and finely sliced
2 garlic cloves, peeled and crushed
1 small lemon, finely sliced
½ lemon, juiced
1 tsp capers, finely chopped
250ml chicken stock
Small bunch of parsley, finely sliced
Salt and pepper to season
300g tuna steak, cut into thin slices
80g Parmesan, grated (optional)

1 Pour the oil into a pan and add the shallot and garlic. Fry off over a medium heat for 5 minutes.
2 Scatter the lemon slices over the shallots and squeeze in the lemon juice and capers. Cook for 5 minutes.
3 Add the stock to the pan along with the parsley and season with a pinch of salt and twist of pepper.
4 Place a large pan of water on to boil. Once boiling, salt well, add the pasta and cook until *al dente*.
5 Into a small frying pan, add a tablespoon of oil and a small knob of butter. Sear the tuna pieces all over, keeping them pink inside if possible.
6 Drain the pasta, tumble the tubes into the stock and stir.
7 Spoon into bowls and add a few strips of tuna to the top of each dish.
8 If feeling brave, add a sprinkle of Parmesan and enjoy.

AOSTA VALLEY

VALLE D'AOSTA

'Aosta' is the capital of this, the smallest region of Italy with the smallest population. A stunningly beautiful mountainous region in the northwest of the country, the region's borders include, France, Switzerland, the Alps and Piedmont. Aosta Valley takes its influences from both France and Germany in both language and cuisine, with French recognised as one of the official languages of the region.

▲ This rural wooden facade in the town of Rhemes Notre Dame in Valle d'Aosta has a distinctly alpine feel.

▶ The church of the Virgin Mary in Rhemes Notre Dame, Valle d'Aosta sits at the foot of a rugged hillside.

In the kitchens of Valle d'Aosta you will always smell the aroma of warming butter, soft freshly cooked polenta, fragrant cheeses and slow-cooked beef dishes, but the use of pasta is not as popular as it is in other regions of Italy. This just goes to show how different each region of Italy is in terms of cuisine. The people of the Aosta Valley have an ongoing love affair with grains. I have used a combination of different flours in this regional chapter, from '00' flour to rye and kamut flour, to provide a filling and comforting dish every time.

TAGLIOLINI PASTA WITH TROUT

TAGLIOLINI ALLA TROTA

I grew up on a farm, where we as a family were lucky to have a fully stocked trout lake along with some perch, roach and carp. If trout was on the menu, my mum would ask my sister Daniela and I to grab our fishing rods (which were long sticks with a short line and hook) and go and catch our dinner. Here, use your favourite fish; if you can source trout, or even better catch a rainbow trout, then a bowl of comfort awaits you.

Preparation time 15 minutes
Cooking time 30 minutes
Serves 4

———

400g *tagliolini* pasta
2 tbsp olive oil
30g unsalted butter
1 garlic clove, peeled and finely sliced
4 leaves of sage, shredded
2 trout, filleted, skinned and chopped
    into chunks
100ml white wine (or vermouth)
500g passata
Salt and pepper to season
Small handful of celery leaves,
    finely sliced
40g Parmesan, grated (optional)

1 Into a shallow sauté pan, pour the olive oil and butter. Melt over a low heat and add the garlic and sage leaves. Stir with a wooden spoon and cook for 2 minutes.

2 Add the trout fillet chunks to the pan and stir. Fry off over a medium heat for 5 minutes then add the white wine and reduce for 1 minute.

3 Pour in the passata, season with salt and pepper and scatter over the celery leaves. Cook for 15 minutes.

4 Place a large pan of water on to boil for the *tagliolini*. Once boiling, salt the water well and cook the pasta until *al dente*. Drain the pasta (reserving a ladle of pasta water).

5 Add the delicate pasta ribbons to the trout sauce and stir. Pour a little of the pasta water in if required. This will loosen the sauce but also it will aid in emulsifying it.

6 Serve with a sprinkle of grated Parmesan.

CARMELA'S TIPS
Spaghetti can also be used, as can linguine, if preferred.

———

DITALINI PASTA WITH FAVA BEANS AND A NICE CHIANTI

DITALINI CON FAVE E FONTINA

All of my favourite ingredients in one dish! Pasta, beans, bread and cheese – clearly this dish will lead to complete tummy satisfaction. Now, I'm a lover of tinned and frozen beans, not only for my store cupboard's peace of mind but also for ease, speed and my sanity.

Preparation time 10 minutes
Cooking time 30 minutes
Serves 4

400g *ditalini* (small pasta tubes)
2 tbsp olive oil
25g unsalted butter
1 shallot, peeled and finely sliced
1 garlic clove, peeled and finely sliced
500g passata
180g fava (broad) beans
   (I use frozen beans)
Small bunch of basil, roughly torn
Salt and pepper to season
150g stale bread, cut into small cubes
200g fontina cheese, cut into thin slices

1 Put the olive oil and 5g of butter into a shallow saucepan along with the sliced shallot and garlic. Fry off gently over a medium heat for 3 minutes.
2 Pour in the tomato passata along with the fava beans and half the basil. Stir and season with salt and pepper.
3 Place a large pan of water on to boil. Once boiling, salt well and add the pasta. Cook the *ditalini* until *al dente*.
4 Place the stale bread cubes in a small frying pan with the remaining 20g of butter and lightly toast.
5 Drain the pasta and tumble the tubes into the sauce. Scatter over the fontina slices and remaining basil.
6 Stir and spoon into a large warmed serving dish. Sprinkle over the toasted cubes of bread to finish.

GNOCCHI WITH SLOW-COOKED VENISON

GNOCCHI AL RAGU DI CERVO

The northern regions of Italy love polenta and gnocchi more than pasta. So I give you a slow-cooked venison sugo with scrumptious pillows of potato and wholewheat flour. When I think of gnocchi I immediately think of the autumn: warming and comforting. Gnocchi can simply be served with a wild mushroom sugo (sauce) or a delicious gorgonzola cream sauce or one of many other options. It is incredibly versatile and inexpensive when paired with seasonal ingredients.

Preparation time 1 hour
Cooking time 1 hour 30 minutes
Serves 4

FOR THE GNOCCHI
1kg potatoes (Maris Piper)
225g kamut flour
2 large eggs
Pinch of freshly grated nutmeg
70g Parmesan, grated
Twist of salt and pepper to season
Small bunch of parsley, finely chopped

FOR THE SUGO
1 tbsp olive oil
30g unsalted butter
1 shallot, peeled and finely chopped
1 carrot, peeled and finely chopped
1 small celery stick, cut into small cubes
1 garlic clove, peeled and crushed
800g venison, cut into small
   bite-sized pieces
125ml white wine
1 tbsp tomato purée
1 sprig of rosemary
1 bay leaf
1 sprig of thyme
Salt and pepper to season
300ml chicken stock
60g Parmesan, grated

1 Start by making the sugo. Take a large shallow pan and add the oil and butter. Over a medium heat gently cook the shallot, carrot, celery and garlic for 10 minutes until softened.
2 Tumble in the venison, stir and sear all over.
3 Pour in the white wine and squeeze in the tomato purée. Stir and add the fresh herbs.
4 Add half the stock and stir. Cook for 1 hour until tender. Add more stock at intervals during cooking if required. Season with salt and pepper.
5 Meanwhile, to make the gnocchi, boil the potatoes with their skins on until tender.
6 Once cooled a little, peel the potatoes and rice them through a potato ricer.
7 Into a large bowl, add the potatoes, flour, eggs, nutmeg, Parmesan, salt and pepper. Incorporate fully to form a dough.
8 Place the dough on a wooden board and knead for 1 minute. Wrap the gnocchi dough in cling film and rest for 15 minutes.
9 Lightly flour a wooden board and portion the dough into four pieces.
10 Roll out each portion into long sausages, the thickness of your middle finger.
11 Cut the sausages into small pieces, 3cm in length. Roll the gnocchi gently down a fork or gnocchi board (or butter pat) to make them *rigate* (ridged), if desired (however, this is not essential). Place the gnocchi on a tray dusted with polenta and finish the remaining gnocchi.
12 Stir and check the venison for seasoning, and if required more stock.
13 Place a large pan of water on to boil. Once boiling, salt well and tumble the gnocchi into the water. Cook until the gnocchi float to the top. They may need to be cooked in batches or use two pans, if it's easier.
14 Remove the sprig of rosemary, bay leaf and thyme from the venison, ensuring that any wooden stems have been removed.

15 Using a slotted spoon, remove the gnocchi from the water and drop them into the venison sugo.

16 Stir the pan to incorporate fully. Add a little water from the gnocchi if needed.

17 Sprinkle in 30g Parmesan and stir.

18 Serve with an additional sprinkle of Parmesan and the chopped parsley.

POLENTA GNOCCHI

GNOCCHI DI POLENTA

Unlike the southern regions, Valle d'Aosta doesn't boast many pasta dishes. However, due to the climate and mountainous surroundings, polenta is available at many a family table along with an array of meat, game and a wide selection of dairy produce. This is an example of *cucina povera* cooking in the mountains. I've included these polenta gnocchi because they are different to the gnocchi you already know and love. I tend to serve these with oven-roasted seasonal vegetables, a basket of bread and glass or two of wine. Equally, it works well as a side dish – warming, comforting and an essential dish from the north of Italy.

———

Preparation tim 10 minutes
Cooking time 20 minutes
Serves 4

———

350g polenta
800ml milk
200ml water
Freshly grated nutmeg
60g unsalted butter
180g fontina
2 egg yolks (save the whites for an
    omelette or meringue)
70g Grana Padano, grated, plus
    extra to serve
Salt and a twist of pepper to season

1 Pour the milk into a non-stick saucepan along with 200ml of water.
2 Bring the saucepan to a light simmer and add the freshly grated nutmeg and 30g of butter.
3 Stir well and once simmering, pour in the polenta and stir. Continue stirring for 5 minutes until the polenta has thickened and has become silky.
4 Remove from the heat. Add the fontina and egg yolks and season with salt and pepper.
5 Using a spatula, scrape the polenta out into a lined baking dish. Allow the polenta to cool down then set by popping it in the fridge for an hour.
6 Preheat the oven to 180°C (gas 4).
7 Using a small glass or pastry cutter, cut circles of polenta (5cm in diameter) and place them into an ovenproof dish with a drizzle of the remaining butter and a sprinkle of Grana Padano. Bake for 20 minutes.
8 Remove from the oven and grill for an additional 5 minutes so that the gnocchi turn a light shade of golden.
9 Serve with additional Grana Padano.

CARMELA'S TIPS
Instead of using water in this recipe, I use the liquid from mozzarella bags made up to 200ml. I always have a jug of mozzarella liquid in the fridge. I love the flavour and this echoes the simplicity that is Italian cooking.

———

RYE FLOUR QUADRETTI PASTA WITH LEEKS AND CHEESE SAUCE

QUADRETTI CON PORRI E TOMA

I adore this dish not only for just its simplicity of course but for the indulgent yet light cheese and cream-based sauce. Pasta in this region tends to be made with a combination of '00' flour and either chestnut or rye flour, providing a filling yet robust pasta.

Preparation time 1 hour
Cooking time 25 minutes
Serves 4

———

FOR THE PASTA DOUGH
260g '00' flour
130g rye flour
4 large eggs

FOR THE SAUCE
1 tbsp olive oil
50g unsalted butter
1 large leek, washed, trimmed,
    finely sliced
150ml double cream
150ml milk
300g toma cheese (regional
    semi-fat cheese)
Salt and pepper to season
Small bunch of parsley,
    roughly chopped

1 Mix both flours together and tip them onto a wooden board. Make a well in the centre and crack in the eggs. Incorporate the flour and eggs gently with your fingertips or with the aid of a fork. Roll into a dough and knead for 5–7 minutes until smooth and elastic.

2 Wrap the dough in cling film and allow to rest for a minimum of 30 minutes.

3 Roll the pasta using either a pasta machine or rolling pin until the dough is silky and a thickness of approximately 4mm.

4 Using a sharp knife or pastry cutter, cut the pasta into diamonds approximately 5cm x 4cm. Allow the pasta to dry a little while you prepare the sauce.

5 Into a sauté pan, add the oil, butter and leek and gently soften the leeks over a medium heat. Stir well and season with a little salt and pepper. Cook for 10–15 minutes.

6 Place a glass bowl over a saucepan of simmering water to create a bain-marie, ensuring the glass bowl doesn't touch the water.

7 Pour the cream into the glass bowl along with the milk and roughly chopped toma cheese.

8 Stir until the cheese has fully melted. Add a twist of black pepper.

9 Place a large pan of water on to boil. Once boiling, salt well and cook the pasta until *al dente*.

10 Drain the pasta and add it into the buttered leeks and stir.

11 Remove the pasta and leeks from the heat and stir in the toma sauce and half the parsley. Combine fully and check for additional seasoning.

12 Serve in warm bowls with an additional sprinkle of parsley.

CARMELA'S TIP
If toma cheese is a little tricky to come by, use a combination of fontina and taleggio.

———

BASILICATA

Basilicata, bordered by both Calabria and Puglia, is one of the poorest regions of Italy. The area has had many lows, such as the evacuation of the city of Matera in the 1950s in order to improve sanitation and renovate the poverty-stricken area. But how things have changed. Matera now has running water and is back in business, a stunning city to visit with views that stretch for miles. Although it is still poor financially and economically the region is rich in many other ways including its cuisine.

Basilicata was always known as and referred to as 'barren land', formed of dry land with very little chance of growing much to sustain one's simple existence. But what did grow in abundance in the piping hot sunshine were hot chilli plants. These would be found nestled in unlikely spots between rocks and could grow anywhere.

No wonder this region is famous for and loves chilli. Potenza is the capital of the region and a province in itself, along with Matera. As far as cooking goes, Matera takes its lead from Puglia whilst Potenza is influenced by Calabria. In a way, Basilicata showcases the best of three regions, with the love of cured meat and pork leading the way. The region has a simple diet encouraging seasonal eating and *cucina povera* cooking.

▲ Handmade *orecchiette*, a typical pasta of Apulia and Basilicata.

▶ Matera lies in the remote southern region of Basilicata, still little-visited by foreign travellers. It is a town famous to fellow Italians for its extensive cave-dwelling districts, the *sassi*.

BAKED ORECCHIETTE WITH MEATBALLS AND MOZZARELLA

ORECCHIETTE AL FORNO

I find baked pasta dishes incredibly comforting, especially when you can see a meatball or two peeping through. Effortless to prepare, this dish would suit most short pasta shapes. Sauce the dish well and if you're feeling adventurous, add a couple of chopped boiled eggs.

Preparation time 1 hour
Cooking time 20 minutes
Serves 4

500g *orecchiette*, freshly prepared (page 29) or dried
1 quantity of meatballs (page 72)

FOR THE SUGO

2 tbsp olive oil
2 garlic cloves, peeled and finely sliced
2 x 400g tins chopped tomatoes
80g green olives, stoned and quartered
1 small red chilli, finely chopped
Small bunch of parsley, roughly chopped
Pinch of dried oregano
Small bunch of basil, roughly torn
Salt and pepper to season
300g mozzarella, torn into pieces
125g pecorino, grated

1 Prepare the meatballs as described on page 72.

2 Once the meatballs have been made and fried, prepare the sugo.

3 Pour the olive oil into a large pan and over a low heat gently fry the garlic for 3 minutes.

4 Add the tinned tomatoes and meatballs and stir.

5 Tumble in the olives and add the chilli, parsley, oregano and half the basil.

6 Stir and season with salt and pepper.

7 Cook over a medium heat for 30 minutes.

8 Preheat the oven to 180°C (gas 4).

9 Place a large pan of water on to boil. Once boiling, salt well, add the *orecchiette* and cook until *al dente*.

10 Drain the pasta then tip it back into the same pan.

11 Add the sauce and meatballs to the pasta. Stir and scatter through the mozzarella and half the grated pecorino cheese. Stir once more.

12 Spoon the pasta into an ovenproof dish and sprinkle over the remaining pecorino cheese. Bake for 20 minutes until the mozzarella has melted. Serve with a final scattering of basil.

LAGANE WITH CHICKPEAS
LAGANE E CECI

Basilicata is a region of simplicity when it comes to cooking. Please do not be disappointed when I tell you that I tend to cheat with this recipe as I use tinned chickpeas for speed and urgency. If time and patience allow, then used dried chickpeas, soak them overnight in water, drain and cook for at least 3 hours. *Lagane* is a long wide pasta that can easily be replaced with *pappardelle*.

Preparation time 10 minutes
Cooking time 40 minutes
Serves 4

FOR THE PASTA
400g '00' flour
1 large egg
200ml water

FOR THE CHICKPEAS
5 tbsp olive oil
2 garlic cloves, peeled and crushed
2 banana shallots, finely sliced
450g tin chickpeas
Salt and pepper to season
1 small chilli, finely chopped
Small bunch of basil, torn
Small sprig of fresh thyme,
    roughly chopped
40g Parmesan (optional)

1 To make *lagane* by hand, tip the flour onto a board and make a well in the centre.
2 Add the egg and half the water to the well and using a fork or your fingertips if preferred, begin to incorporate the flour and water, slowly adding a little more as required. Form into a ball and knead for 5 minutes until elastic and smooth.
3 Cover and allow to rest for 30 minutes.
4 Roll out the dough with a rolling pin to a thin sheet the thickness of a 10p coin.
5 Using a pastry wheel, cut the pasta into 2.5cm strips around 15cm long. Allow them to dry for about 20 minutes before cooking.
6 Place a large pan of water on to boil. Once boiling, salt well and add the pasta. Cook the *lagane* until *al dente*.
7 Pour the olive oil into a large sauté pan and bring to a medium heat. Add the garlic and shallots. Cook gently until translucent.
8 Add the chickpeas to the onion and season with salt, pepper and fresh chilli. Stir.
9 Scatter the basil and thyme into the chickpeas and stir.
10 Drain the pasta, reserving 30ml of the water. Add the pasta and reserved water to the chickpeas, stir well and serve with an optional grating of Parmesan.

HOT BUCATINI

BUCATINI PICANTE

Do you like it hot? If so, how hot? Basilicatans love the heat of chilli in their pasta and food in general. These chillies pop through the driest of soil with the help of the hot southern sun. You have been warned! Be sure to serve with a large jug of water.

Preparation time 5 minutes
Cooking time 12 minutes
Serves 4

400g *bucatini*
125ml olive oil
3 garlic cloves, peeled and halved
5 red chillies, whole
Salt to season
5 large basil leaves, roughly torn
Small bunch of parsley, finely chopped

1 Place a large pan of water on to boil. Once boiling, salt well and add the *bucatini*. Cook the pasta according to the packet instructions, minus 2 minutes to ensure it remains *al dente*.
2 Pour 80ml of oil into a small frying pan and add the whole chillies and garlic. Fry them off gently for around 5 minutes, taking care to not burn the garlic as it will catch very easily.
3 Gently spoon the oil, chillies and garlic into a food processor and blitz until smooth for 30 seconds.
4 Add the remaining oil to the frying pan over a low heat and scrape in the chilli mixture.
5 Drain the *bucatini*, reserving 50ml of the starchy pasta water.
6 Add the *bucatini* to the chilli mixture and stir in the reserved pasta water. Stir well to incorporate the fiery mixture fully.
7 Scatter over the basil and parsley and serve in warm bowls with a large glass of water.

SIMPLE SPAGHETTI
SPAGHETTI ALLA SAN GIOVANNI

This spaghetti dish would be one that I would choose to make as a speedy supper. It's the kind of dish I would cook on a night when I have limited energy and think 'takeaway', or when all of my four children are chirping like little birds that need feeding immediately. This dish would be on the table within 20 minutes and bowls would be licked clean within 2 minutes. It's just delicious.

———————

Preparation time 5 minutes
Cooking time 20 minutes
Serves 4

———————

400g dried spaghetti
3 tbsp olive oil
2 garlic cloves, peeled and finely sliced
2 anchovies, in oil, drained
1 x 400g tin plum tomatoes
25g capers, roughly chopped
60g black olives, stoned and
    roughly chopped
1 small red chilli, deseeded and finely
    chopped
Small bunch of parsley, roughly chopped
Pinch of oregano
Salt and pepper to season
70g pecorino, grated (optional)

1 Pour the olive oil into a sauté or shallow pan.
2 Add the garlic and fry off on a low heat for 3 minutes.
3 Tumble in the drained anchovies and stir.
4 Pour in the plum tomatoes and break them up with the back of a wooden spoon. Tumble in the capers, olives, chilli and half the parsley.
5 Stir, sprinkle in the oregano and season with salt and pepper. Cook for 20 minutes.
6 Place a large pan of water on to boil for the spaghetti. Once boiling, salt well.
7 Add the spaghetti, cook and drain when *al dente*.
8 Add the spaghetti to the sauce along with the remaining parsley. Stir and serve with an optional scattering of pecorino.

TAGLIOLINI IN STOCK WITH DELICATE MEATBALLS

TAGLIOLINI IN BRODO CON POLPETTINE

The pairing of pasta and meatballs screams 'eat me, Carmela' and represents the finest in comfort food. I also love this recipe because you gain a second meat course. Making the stock yourself leaves you with the chicken and lamb to have after or alongside your pasta dish. The flavour of freshly made stock as it permeates through the house reminds me of what my mum would call 'children's medicine' – the remedy for anything and everything, especially when tiny *pastina* stars or broken *spaghettini* were added.

Preparation time 1 hour
Cooking time 2 hours
Serves 4

350g *tagliolini* or spaghetti

FOR THE STOCK
300g chicken, breast or on-the-bone pieces
300g lamb chunks
1 large onion, skin on and quartered
2 large garlic cloves, skin on and halved
1 celery stick, plus leaves, roughly chopped
3 large ripe tomatoes, quartered
1 large carrot, unpeeled and roughly chopped
Bunch of parsley with stalks
Salt and pepper to season

FOR THE MEATBALLS
150g veal mince
150g pork mince
1 garlic clove, peeled and crushed
1 egg
80g dried breadcrumbs
Small bunch of parsley, finely chopped
Pinch of dried chilli
Pinch of marjoram
Salt and pepper to season
Olive oil, for frying
60g pecorino, grated

1 Start by making the perfect stock. Into a large heavy-bottomed saucepan, add all of the stock ingredients and top with cold water (4 pints).
2 Cook the stock for around 2 hours, checking and seasoning halfway through.
3 To make the meatballs, place the veal and pork mince into a bowl with the garlic, egg and breadcrumbs. Mix with a wooden spoon.
4 Scatter in the parsley, chilli and marjoram. Season with salt and pepper and make sure everything is fully incorporated.
5 Roll into small balls, just a little smaller than a walnut (the smaller the better really, if patience and hunger allow).
6 Heat a little olive oil in a pan and fry the meatballs in batches, placing them on kitchen towels to remove excess oil, until coloured all over and almost cooked through.
7 Remove the chicken and lamb from the stock and set aside for your second course.
8 Strain the stock through a sieve and into a clean pan. Using the back of a wooden spoon, push the remaining vegetables through the sieve making sure the flavour ends up in the clean pan and not in the sieve. Scrape the base of the sieve into the pan and discard any vegetable remains.
9 Bring the stock back to a gentle simmer and add the meatballs. Cook the meatballs for 15 minutes, checking the stock for seasoning.
10 Add the pasta to the stock and cook until *al dente*.
11 Serve in warm bowls with a sprinkle of pecorino.

CALABRIA

Calabria is found at the southern-most point of Italy, directly opposite Sicily, with Catanzaro as its capital. This spicy region borders the barren but enticing Basilicata, and the coastline kisses both the Tyrrhenian Sea to the west and the Ionian Sea to the east.

▲ *Pallone di fichi* (fig balls) from Cosenza, Calabria, in southern Italy.

▶ The medieval city of Gerace in Calabria.

When I think back to Calabria I can almost smell the aroma from the sea, feel the heat from the afternoon sun on my face and taste the chilli heat from the warm bowl of *pasta con 'nduja* that I'd be tucking into.

Cucina povera cooking echoes through each province of Calabria, along with a sense of pride and individuality: simple spaghetti dishes to hand-rolled pasta, large pasta *paccheri* tubes, pasta with chickpeas and a Calabrese feast in the way of a classic lasagne known as *sagne chine*. This is an incredibly delicious region boasting the likes of the wonderful UK-based chef Francesco Mazzei, a great inspiration of mine and now fronting Sartoria restaurant in London, whose native roots are still at the forefront of his cooking.

FESTIVAL LASAGNE CALABRESE STYLE

SAGNE CHINE

Filled and layered pasta is the symbol of a classic Italian Sunday lunch, but lasagne in Italy varies tremendously from region to region. This version from Calabria does remind me a little of my mum Solidea's version from Molise, but it's packed with even more delights. Although normally made on a celebration day, with a little forward planning, this is the kind of dish I prepare most Sunday lunchtimes.

Preparation time 1 hour
Cooking time 1 hour 30 minutes
Serves 6

600g lasagne sheets

FOR THE MEATBALLS
200g pork mince
200g beef mince
200g veal mince
2 garlic cloves, peeled and crushed
1 egg and 1 yolk
100g dried breadcrumbs
Small bunch of parsley, finely chopped
1 tsp dried oregano
Pinch of dried chilli
Salt and pepper to season
Olive oil, for frying

FOR THE MEATBALL SAUCE
2 tbsp olive oil
1 small onion, peeled and finely diced
1 small carrot, peeled and finely diced
1 celery stick, finely diced
2 garlic cloves, peeled and crushed
2 x 675g bottles passata
200ml water
1 tbsp tomato purée
Salt and pepper to season
Bunch of fresh basil, torn

1 Start by making the meatballs. These can be made in advance and frozen to save time. Place the pork, beef and veal mince into a large bowl and use a wooden spoon to break up the mince.

2 Add in the garlic, whole egg and yolk. Stir.

3 Tumble in the breadcrumbs, parsley, chilli, oregano, salt and pepper. I tend to get my hands into the meat mix to ensure everything has been fully incorporated.

4 Now you need to roll the meat into tiny meatballs, just a little bigger that a marble. Mine are completely uneven, so please don't worry too much about making them perfect.

5 Once the meatballs are ready, heat some olive oil and fry them off in batches. Once coloured all over, allow them to drain on kitchen roll.

6 To prepare the sauce, take a large pan. Pour in the olive oil and over a medium heat fry off the onion, carrot and celery for 5 minutes until softened.

7 Add the garlic and stir.

8 Pour in the passata and water. Stir well and squeeze in the tomato purée and add the basil.

9 Gently add the meatballs to the sauce and cook for 2 hours over a medium heat.

10 Preheat the oven to 180°C (gas 4).

11 Take a large bakeware dish, about 30cm x 20cm; make sure it has a good depth too.

12 Ladle in some sauce and spread over the base ensuring a light covering all over.

13 Take the lasagne sheets and cover the base and sides of the bakeware dish. Do not overlap the pasta but just ensure there are no gaps.

14 Cover the base layer of pasta with a ladle of the meatball sauce, followed by a sprinkle of sliced eggs, a handful of peas, mushrooms and mozzarella and a dusting of pecorino. Spoon over a tiny amount of sauce.

FOR THE FILLING
5 boiled eggs, peeled and thinly sliced
300g peas
200g mushrooms, thinly sliced
400g mozzarella, torn into small pieces
150g pecorino, grated

15 Place another layer of lasagne sheets on top of the sauce (but not the sides of the dish). Repeat with the filling and sauce, so you have at least three layers.

16 For the final layer, if there are any sheets of lasagne hanging over from the base, fold them over and top with more lasagne sheets, sauce and a sprinkle of pecorino and mozzarella.

17 Cover with foil and bake in the preheated oven for an hour and a half. Remove the foil after an hour and bake with no covering for the final 30 minutes.

18 Once cooked, remove from the oven, cover and allow to rest for 15 minutes before slicing.

FILEJA (FUSILLI) WITH 'NDUJA AND SUNDRIED TOMATOES

FILEJA CON 'NDUJA E POMODORI SECCE

I'm not sure you can visit Calabria without trying its much loved 'nduja salami. 'Nduja is a spreadable spicy pork salami that's incredibly versatile. It's delicious slathered over bread or as part of your antipasti starters, but I simply adore using it in pasta dishes. 'Nduja has a rich warm flavour from chillies and a depth of flavour from deliciously cured pork. An essential to any Calabrese store cupboard, *fileja* is also known as fusilli and is made in the south of Italy using a *ferro*, as described on page 30.

Preparation time 10 minutes
Cooking time 30 minutes
Serves 4

400g *fileja* pasta
2 tbsp olive oil
1 garlic clove, peeled and crushed
150g pancetta, cubed
100g 'nduja
70g sundried tomatoes, finely sliced
30g olives, pitted and finely sliced
1 tbsp tomato purée
1 x 400g tin plum tomatoes
Large bunch of basil, roughly torn
Salt and pepper to season
100g pecorino, grated

---

1 Pour the olive oil into a sauté pan and add the garlic. Gently fry off for one minute then add the pancetta and stir. Cook for 5–7 minutes then tumble in the 'nduja, sundried tomatoes, olives and tomato purée.

2 Stir well. Add a tin of plum tomatoes followed by half the fresh basil and a good twist of salt and pepper. Cook on a low heat for 20 minutes. Check for seasoning after 10 minutes.

3 Place a large pan of water onto boil for the pasta. Once boiling, salt well, add the pasta and cook until *al dente*.

4 Drain the pasta, reserving a small ladle of starchy water.

5 Add the pasta to the sauce with the ladle of pasta water. Stir well to incorporate.

6 Add the remaining basil and 30g of pecorino. Stir and serve in warm bowls with an additional sprinkle of pecorino if required.

SMALL LASAGNE WITH CHICKPEAS

PASTA CON CECI

The simplicity of the south in one warming, filling dish – not much beats *cucina povera* cooking in my opinion. If you choose to be a purist, soak your chickpeas overnight in a little bicarbonate of soda and water, but the tinned kind are fine. The handmade pasta can easily be replaced with any short pasta of your choice to save time too. I also love to combine both cannellini beans and chickpeas.

Preparation time 1 hour
Cooking time 25 minutes
Serves 4

400g prepared egg pasta dough
    (page 13)
Polenta, for dusting
4 tbsp olive oil
1 onion, peeled and finely chopped
2 garlic cloves, peeled and crushed
1 bay leaf
800g fresh tomatoes, skinned, pulp only
1 tbsp tomato purée
650g tinned chickpeas, drained
    and rinsed
Small handful of celery leaves,
    finely chopped
2 fronds wild fennel, finely chopped
Salt and pepper to season
1 small chilli, deseeded and finely sliced
Small bunch of basil, roughly torn
100g Parmesan, grated

1 Roll the pasta dough out with a pasta machine or rolling pin into lasagne sheets. Using a knife, cut the lasagne sheets into 5cm x 5cm pieces.
2 Place them on a tray dusted with polenta whilst you prepare the sauce.
3 Pour the olive oil into a large sauté pan. Over a medium heat, add the onion and cook until just translucent.
4 Add the garlic, bay leaf and tomato pulp. Cook for 5 minutes.
5 Squeeze in the tomato purée and add the chickpeas.
6 Scatter in the celery leaves and fennel and season with salt and pepper. If you like the heat of a fresh chilli, add it now, then stir.
7 Cook the sauce over a gentle heat for 25 minutes.
8 Place a large pan of water on to boil. Once boiling, salt well, add the pasta and cook until *al dente*.
9 Add the basil to the sauce and check for additional seasoning.
10 Drain the pasta and spoon it into the sauce. Stir before adding half the Parmesan. Serve with an additional sprinkling of Parmesan

PACCHERI WITH SWORDFISH AND BABY PLUM TOMATOES

PACCHERI CON PESCE SPADE E POMODORINI

When I think of Calabria I immediately think of the heat, but I'm referring to the chilli. The Calabrians love their chilli and so do I. In many of my dishes I have given the chilli, fresh or dried, as optional, so that you can make your own choice. In this recipe I have also been inspired by the region's beautiful sea and its contents. In the UK you may need to order your swordfish, so plan ahead if you can.

————

Preparation time 10 minutes
Cooking time 30 minutes
Serves 4

————

400g *paccheri* (large pasta tubes)
4 tbsp olive oil
3 garlic cloves, peeled and crushed
500g swordfish, cut into chunks
500g baby plum tomatoes, quartered
50g olives, pitted and halved
1 small chilli, deseeded and
    finely chopped
Salt and pepper to season
Small bunch of parsley, finely chopped
Small bunch of basil, finely chopped

1 Pour the olive oil into a large shallow pan and add the garlic.
Cook over a low heat for 2 minutes.

2 Add the swordfish chunks to the garlic and cook for 5 minutes.

3 Tumble in the tomatoes, olives and chilli.

4 Stir and cook for an additional 15 minutes until the tomatoes have softened but still hold their shape.

5 Season with salt and pepper.

6 Place a large pan of water on to boil. Once boiling, salt well, add the pasta and cook until *al dente*.

7 Scatter the fresh herbs into the sauce and stir.

8 Drain the pasta and add to the sauce. Stir well and serve.

SPAGHETTI WITH SEASONED BREADCRUMBS

SPAGHETTI ALLA MOLLICA

When you are looking to cook a quick dish but have very little in the fridge, I give you a taste of a Calabrian tradition. This is a flavoursome dish that brings a sense of simplicity and ease to the family table. Who needs a takeaway when this dish can be on the table in 20 minutes?

Preparation time 5 minutes
Cooking time 15 minutes
Serves 4

400g dried spaghetti
4 tbsp olive oil
2 garlic cloves, peeled and crushed
5 large salted tinned anchovies
Salt and pepper to season
1 small chilli, deseeded and finely sliced
20g unsalted butter
100g stale breadcrumbs
Small bunch of basil, finely chopped
Zest of 1 small lemon

1 Place a large pan of water on to boil. Once boiling, salt well and cook the spaghetti until *al dente*.
2 Pour the olive oil into a sauté pan and fry off the garlic for 2 minutes over a low heat. Brush the excess salt off the anchovies with a damp cloth and pat dry with kitchen towel. Add the anchovies to the pan and stir until they have melted away.
3 Season with a pinch of chilli, salt and pepper.
4 Put the butter into another frying pan, add the stale breadcrumbs and lightly toast for 5 minutes.
5 Remove the breadcrumbs from the heat and place them in a bowl with the basil and lemon zest.
6 Drain the spaghetti and reserve 30ml of pasta water. Return the pasta to the cooking pan and add the anchovy mix. Stir well and add the reserved pasta water.
7 Add half the breadcrumb mix and stir.
8 Spoon into bowls and top with an additional breadcrumb topping if desired.

CARMELA'S TIPS
Don't tell anyone, but I love Parmesan with this dish. As a rule, Italians don't serve cheese with fish, however in the UK, and in my kitchen, I think that's down to taste and preference. Have a small bowl ready grated on the table just in case you invite me over for dinner. You can substitute the spaghetti with vermicelli if preferred.

CAMPANIA

Welcome to the hustle and bustle of the second-most highly populated region of Italy. Boasting a luscious coastline, mild climate, warm sunshine and some of the best food Italy has on offer, Campania brings you the stunning and I believe tear-jerkingly beautiful Amalfi coast with its breath-taking views over the sea as well as quaint towns perched above the coast.

Naples is the capital of this region and I have to admit it is one of my favourite capitals, I'm not really sure why, but I think to me this is the real Italy when it comes to both food and a somewhat rugged lifestyle. Naples offers a look into the back streets of Italian life, the raw side, full of workers, strangely photographic washing lines and children's laughter. Then there's the other side of the city, offering high-end clothes and retail stores, mouth-watering restaurants and some of the best places from which to pick up a coffee on the run.

▲ The Amalfi coast, in Campania, is famed for its lemons.

▶ The Royal Palace of Caserta, Campania, was constructed for the Bourbon kings of Naples. It is one of the largest palaces erected in Europe during the 18th century.

Campania instantly brings to mind the best pizza and calzone, as well as some of the best pasta – from Gragnano. Campania is famous for spaghetti, soft handmade mozzarella, amazing tomato sauces and pizza margherita (tomato, mozzarella and basil) named after Queen Margherita, plus some of the best cakes and sweets you can imagine!

CANNELLONI WITH SPINACH, RICOTTA AND A TWIST OF NUTMEG
CANNELLONI CON SPINACHI E RICOTTA

Cannelloni means it must be Sunday. In fact, any filled pasta would normally be served on a Sunday when I was a child. A steaming hot dish would be offered and placed on the centre of our family table. I always remember my lovely mum asking my dad, 'How many cannelloni would you like Roc?' My dad would always reply thirteen! I know, so many, unlucky for some but not for my dad. Lasagne, filled pasta shells or cannelloni – I love them all equally.

Preparation time 1 hour
Cooking time 1 hour 30 minutes
Serves 4

FOR THE PASTA
300g fresh lasagne sheets

FOR THE TOMATO SAUCE
3 tbsp olive oil
1 small onion, peeled and finely diced
1 stick celery, finely diced
1 small carrot, peeled and finely diced
2 garlic cloves, peeled and crushed
1 tbsp tomato purée
800g passata
100ml water
Pinch of chilli flakes (optional)
Small bunch of basil, torn by hand
Salt and pepper to season
Parmesan rind (optional)
70g Parmesan, grated

FOR THE FILLING
450g spinach
800g ricotta
½ tsp freshly grated nutmeg
150g Parmesan, grated, plus 50g for sprinkling
½ tsp dried marjoram
Salt and pepper to season
10 basil leaves, roughly torn

CARMELA'S TIPS
You can also use the ready-made cannelloni tubes, available in most supermarkets.

1 To make the sauce, pour the olive oil into a saucepan and over a medium heat, fry off the onion, celery and carrot until softened, approximately 10 minutes.

2 Add the garlic to the pan and stir, then the tomato purée and mix well.

3 Pour the passata and the water into the saucepan and stir.

4 Add a sprinkle of chilli flakes, if using, season with salt and pepper and add the basil.

5 If you have a Parmesan rind in your fridge, drop it into the sauce for added flavour as this is a meat-free dish.

6 Cook over a medium heat for an hour.

7 To make the filling, place the spinach in a dry frying pan and wilt for 3 minutes, turning.

8 Lay the spinach onto a clean tea towel and squeeze firmly to remove excess water and moisture. Chop finely.

9 Into a bowl, add the spinach, ricotta, nutmeg, 150g Parmesan, marjoram and a twist of salt and pepper. Sprinkle in the basil leaves, stir and taste for seasoning.

10 Preheat the oven to 180°C (gas 4).

11 Spread a ladleful of the tomato sauce over the base of a large ovenproof dish.

12 Cut the lasagne sheets in half. Take 5 teaspoons of filling and place them on the centre of the lasagne sheet and roll the sheet into a sausage.

13 Place the cannelloni in the oven dish and repeat. Tightly pack the cannelloni.

14 Spoon over three ladles of the tomato sauce and add a final sprinkle of Parmesan to the dish.

15 Cover the dish with foil and bake for 40 minutes. After 40 minutes remove the foil and cook for another 15 minutes.

16 Remove from the oven, allow to rest for 10 minutes and serve.

PACCHERI WITH A NEAPOLITAN MEAT SAUCE

PACCHERI CON IL RAGU ALLA NAPOLETANA

Paccheri is one of my favourite pasta shapes, large cylindrical tubes that flatten once cooked, yet have the benefit of housing delicious sauces very well. The large tubes need a heavy meaty sauce and this Napoletana sugo does the job perfectly. Use the sauce recipe as a guide – you can easily substitute the pancetta for *guanciale*, or the rump steak for topside or even chunks of pork fillet. Just remember to cook the sugo long and slow.

Preparation time 25 minutes
Cooking time 3 hours
Serves 4

400g *paccheri*
4 tbsp olive oil
1 small onion, peeled and finely chopped
2 garlic cloves, peeled and finely sliced
125g pancetta, roughly chopped
500g pork ribs
200g soft Italian sausage, roughly chopped
500g rump steak, cut into small chunks
1 large glass red wine
2 tbsp tomato purée
3 x 400g tins chopped tomatoes
100ml chicken stock
1 small chilli, seeds removed and finely chopped
Small bunch of parsley, chopped
Small bunch of basil, torn by hand
Salt and pepper to season
Pinch of oregano (optional)
70g Parmesan, grated

1 Pour 2 tablespoons of olive oil into a large pan and gently fry off the onion, garlic and pancetta on a low heat, until the pancetta has just coloured, around 5 minutes.

2 Remove the onions, garlic and pancetta from the pan and set aside.

3 Add another 2 tablespoons of olive oil to the pan and tumble in the pork ribs, sausage and rump steak chunks. Stir and sear the meat all over; this may take about 10 minutes or so.

4 Tumble the onions, garlic and pancetta back into the pan with the browned meat. Stir and pour in the red wine and tomato purée. Reduce the red wine for 3 minutes then add the tinned tomatoes and stock and season with salt and pepper.

5 If you like a little heat, add the freshly chopped chilli and stir. Scatter in half the parsley and basil. I like to add a pinch of dried oregano too.

6 Stir, cover and allow to cook over a gentle heat for 2 hours 30 minutes.

7 Check the sauce for seasoning.

8 Cook the *paccheri* in a large pan of salted water according to the packet instructions, minus 2 minutes to ensure the pasta remains *al dente*.

9 Once the sauce is ready, I like to pull the meat off the ribs, but you can serve the ribs alongside the pasta in a separate bowl if you prefer.

10 Drain the pasta, add a little sauce and stir with half the Parmesan cheese.

11 Serve in bowls with a topping of the meaty Napoletana sauce and an additional sprinkling of Parmesan. Serve with a full-bodied red wine.

CARMELA'S TIPS
Prepare and make the sauce a day in advance to speed things up at dinner time.

PASTA AND LENTILS
PASTA E LENTICCHIE

Straight from the southern town of Campagna to your family table. This dish echoes *cucina povera* cooking, the essence of simplicity. This recipe is one where I would say pretty much any short pasta shape goes, but I'd recommend *pasta mista*, broken spaghetti, *vermicelli* or *capellini*. The scrumptious lentils make this the perfect warming one-pot dish.

————

1 Pour 3 tablespoons of olive oil into a large pan and gently fry off the onion, celery and pancetta. Fry for approximately 10 minutes then add the garlic and cook for a further minute or so.

2 Sprinkle the lentils into the pan along with the tomato purée and stir.

3 Pour in the water and tinned tomatoes. Stir and add a pinch of chilli, if desired, half the fresh herbs and all of the celery leaves. Season with salt and pepper and cook for 40 minutes until tender. At this stage, if I have a Parmesan rind in my fridge I would drop it into the lentils for the remaining cooking time. I love the flavour that the rind releases even over a short cooking time. This, however, isn't essential.

4 Five minutes before the lentils are ready, add the pasta to the lentils and stir, making sure the bottom of the pan is clear and nothing is sticking. If a little more water is required, add it now. Cook the pasta until *al dente*. Remove the celery stalks and discard as this was used for flavour only.

5 Finish with a sprinkle of fresh herbs. Ladle into bowls with a drizzle of extra virgin olive oil and a sprinkle of Parmesan. Who gets to nibble the softened Parmesan rind? Well, that's up to you.

Preparation time 10 minutes
Cooking time 45 minutes
Serves 4

————

400g *pasta mista* (mixed pasta)
4 tbsp olive oil
1 small onion, peeled and finely diced
1 stick celery, halved
100g pancetta, chopped roughly
2 garlic cloves, peeled and crushed
250g Castelluccio lentils
1 tbsp tomato purée
1.5 litres water
250g tinned chopped tomatoes
Pinch of chilli flakes (optional)
Small bunch of parsley, finely chopped
Small bunch of basil, torn by hand
Small handful of celery leaves,
    finely chopped
Salt and pepper to season
Parmesan rind (optional if you have one
    in the fridge)
70g Parmesan, grated

CARMELA'S TIPS
For a speedy alternative, use puy lentils
or pre-cooked tinned lentils.

————

BUCATINI WITH ANCHOVIES AND CAPERS

BUCATINI ALLA PUTTANESCA

Puttanesca sounds both naughty and delicious as it rolls off the tongue, but the story behind the meaning is rather interesting. This recipe is what beautiful ladies of the night from Naples would make for their dinners after a busy evening on the town. So, clearly this dish would need to be quick to prepare in order to satisfy a raging hunger deep into the night.

———

Preparation time 5 minutes
Cooking time 10 minutes
Serves 4

———

500g *bucatini*
5 tbsp olive oil
1 garlic clove, peeled and sliced
1 small chilli, seeds removed and
    finely chopped
7 anchovy fillets, drained and chopped
50g salted capers, rinsed
100g pitted olives, halved
2 x 400g tins chopped tomatoes
Salt and pepper to season
Small bunch of basil, roughly torn

1 Place a large pan of water on to boil.

2 Heat the oil in a large frying pan and add the garlic, chilli and anchovies. Cook for 3 minutes.

3 Once the water is bubbling, salt well and add the *bucatini*. Cook according to the packet instructions, minus 1 minute.

4 Add the capers and olives to the garlic mix in the frying pan, stir well and pour in the tinned tomatoes.

5 Season with a pinch of salt and pepper. Add the basil and cook for 10 minutes.

6 Drain the pasta and stir through the sauce. Serve immediately in warm bowls.

SPAGHETTI WITH CLAMS

SPAGHETTI ALLE VONGOLE

Sweet clams combined with spaghetti is one of those Neapolitan combinations that has my taste buds in an absolute uproar, whether cooked in tomato sauce or a white wine variation. I adore both recipes. You can get away with using tinned or jarred clams in the tomato-based sauce if you prefer a shortcut. You are probably terribly appalled I have even suggested this, but give it a go – you might be surprised.

Preparation time 10 minutes
Cooking time 20 minutes
Serves 4

400g dried spaghetti
900g small fresh clams in shells

FOR THE TOMATO SAUCE
4 tbsp olive oil
2 garlic cloves, peeled and finely sliced
1 small chilli, deseeded and finely chopped
1 x 400g tin chopped tomatoes
Small bunch of parsley, roughly chopped
Salt and pepper to season

FOR THE WHITE WINE SAUCE
4 tbsp olive oil
2 garlic cloves, peeled and finely chopped
1 small chilli, seeds removed, finely chopped
250ml white wine or vermouth
Salt and pepper to season
Small bunch of parsley, chopped

1 Wash the clams well in cold water. Ensure all clams are closed and discard any with broken, damaged shells or any that are open.
2 Put the clams into a large shallow pan with a lid. Clamp on the lid and shake well. Allow the clams to cook until all the shells have opened, approximately 6–7 minutes. Any clams that have not opened should be thrown away. Remove half the clams from the shells, leaving half of them still with their shells on. Set aside.
3 Heat the oil in a large frying pan and add the chopped garlic and chilli. Cook gently for 5 minutes on a medium heat.
4 For a tomato sauce, drain the tinned tomatoes through a sieve to remove any excess liquid, add to the garlic and stir.
5 Cook for 20 minutes, season well with salt and black pepper. Add half the parsley and stir. Place a large pan of water on to boil for the pasta, salting the water well once boiling.
6 Add the clams to the tomato sauce and stir.
7 Cook the spaghetti according to the packet instructions, minus 2 minutes to ensure the spaghetti remains *al dente*.
8 Drain the spaghetti, add to the clam sauce and stir through. Sprinkle over the remaining parsley and serve.
9 For a white wine sauce, add the cooked clams to the garlic and chilli in the pan, add the white wine, season with salt and pepper and add half the chopped parsley. Clamp on a lid and shake well.
10 Cook the spaghetti in the boiling water according to the packet instructions, minus 2 minutes to ensure the spaghetti remains *al dente*, with a bite.
11 Drain the spaghetti and add to the clams. Stir thoroughly, add the remaining parsley and serve immediately.

CARMELA'S TIPS
Try vermicelli as a change from traditional spaghetti.

EMILIA-ROMAGNA

Emilia-Romagna, oh where to begin! I have visited the region many times and have fallen very much in love with the overall ambience there, but I also appreciate that this delicious region is defined by two unique entities, Emilia and Romagna. Emilia-Romagna as a whole is nicknamed La Grassa, 'the fat one'. You could never leave this region hungry, it's just not possible, and to be honest the very thought of the region has me salivating. I always remember this quote from the region '*Conti corti e tagliatelle lunghe*', which means 'bills should be short but the pasta long'.

Boasting Bologna as its capital, the gastronomic capital of Italy, Emilia-Romagna is incredibly well known for its pasta, and can they make pasta. Specialising in filled tortellini, rolled *rotolo* filled pasta, stuffed *cappelletti* from Ferrara, hand-rolled *garganelli* and delicate *sorprese*, to name a few. It wasn't until I visited Romagna with my good friend Monica that I discovered and was taught how to make *passatelli*. If there is one recipe that you must try in this region, *Passatelli in brodo* (broth) is the one.

▲ Fresh egg yolk raviolo (see page 96 for the full recipe).

▶ The San Luca arcade in Bologna, Emilia-Romagna, is the longest in the world.

FRESH EGG YOLK RAVIOLO

UOVA DA RAVIOLO

This easy-to-make dish encourages the indulgent side of me to join the dinner table, always wanting more (see page 94 for a photo of the dish). Ideally, this raviolo dish would be served as a starter, one or two per person. However, they can be made slightly smaller to accommodate two or three per person as a main dish.

Preparation time 1 hour
Cooking time 5 minutes
Serves 4 (as a starter)

300g fresh prepared egg pasta dough (page 13)
700g fresh ricotta
100g Parmesan, grated (and optional extra for the table)
½ tsp nutmeg, freshly grated
125g spinach, blanched and finely chopped
Pinch of oregano
Salt and pepper to season
4 large egg yolks
50g butter
12 sage leaves

1 Place the ricotta, Parmesan, nutmeg, spinach, oregano and salt and pepper in a bowl and stir. Taste and check for additional seasoning.
2 Spoon the filling into a disposable piping bag. Clip the top to seal the bag and transfer to the fridge to chill.
3 Roll the pasta dough out into thin lasagne sheets.
4 Cut out eight 10cm circles with a pastry cutter.
5 Pipe a circle of filling on four of the circles, leaving a 1cm gap around the outside perimeter to seal.
6 Drop an egg yolk into the centre of each circle. Using your finger, if required dampen the outside of the pasta disc and seal with another pasta circle to make a complete raviolo.
7 Repeat with the remaining ravioli.
8 Take a large pan of water. Once boiling, salt well.
9 Meanwhile, scrape the butter into a small frying pan and gently brown over a medium heat. Add the sage leaves.
10 Cook the ravioli in the boiling salted water. Normally each raviolo will take about 2 minutes 40 seconds to cook; this will leave you with beautifully cooked pasta and a dippy egg. Cooking the pasta in a very large pan means you will be able to cook four to six at a time.
11 Take out of the pan using a slotted spoon and place the cooked ravioli onto a clean kitchen towel to remove excess water.
12 Gently place each raviolo into a bowl with a drizzle of butter and three sage leaves. Sprinkle with an additional grating of Parmesan, if desired.

CARMELA'S TIPS
Don't waste the egg whites. You can freeze them for use another time in a meringue or egg white omelette.

FRESH TAGLIATELLE WITH A SLOW-COOKED MEAT SAUCE

TAGLIATELLE AL RAGU

Dare I say this is a 'Bolognese' sauce. In Italy this dish is known as *Tagliatelle al ragu*, a slow-cooked meat-based sauce served with leggy fresh tagliatelle, never spaghetti! However, this is always a controversial recipe as it's not set in stone and there is no go-to recipe. I'm sure my version will raise a few eyebrows. Red wine, white wine, chicken livers, milk, yes or no? After much research and a little time in my kitchen, I give you the recipe that I serve to my family.

Preparation time 20 minutes
Cooking time 4 hours
Serves 4

————

400g fresh tagliatelle or dried
2 tbsp olive oil
25g unsalted butter
150g pancetta, cubed
1 small onion, peeled and finely diced
1 stick celery, finely diced
1 small carrot, peeled and finely diced
2 garlic cloves, peeled and crushed
50g chicken livers, finely minced
200g minced beef
200g minced pork
3 tbsp tomato purée
1 large glass red wine (white wine can also be used)
600g passata, plus 150ml water
Small bunch of basil, torn by hand
Salt and pepper to season
70g Parmesan, grated

1 Into a saucepan, over a low heat, melt the olive oil and butter.
2 Add the pancetta and cook for 5 minutes to colour, then add the onion, celery and carrot. Stir well and cook for a further 5 minutes.
3 Add the garlic and chicken livers. Stir and cook for 2 minutes.
4 Add the beef and pork mince. Stir to combine, breaking up any lumps with a wooden spoon. Cook for 5 minutes until the mince is coloured all over.
5 Squeeze in the tomato purée and stir.
6 Now pour in the wine of your choice. I do prefer red as I find the sauce has a richness only found in a deep dry red wine.
7 Stir and allow the wine to reduce by half.
8 Add the passata. I add passata as I prefer a slightly more liquid-based sauce. Stir and add the water (I normally swill out the passata bottle with water). Scatter over basil and season with salt and pepper.
9 Cook over a low heat for 4 hours. If the sauce looks a little dry add a little stock or water.
10 Place a large pan of water on to boil for the tagliatelle. Once boiling, salt the water well.
11 Cook the tagliatelle until *al dente* and drain, reserving a ladle of water.
12 Add the drained tagliatelle to the sauce along with a small ladle of reserved pasta water. Stir and serve with a scattering of grated Parmesan.

CARMELA'S TIPS

If you'd prefer, leave out the chicken livers. I have added no milk to my sauce but if you wish you can add about 100ml of milk just after the mince has browned, replacing the water.

PASSATELLI IN STOCK
PASSATELLI IN BRODO

Nonna Violante (aged seventy-six) from Hotel Eliseo in Romagna taught me how to make *passatelli* by hand whilst I was on a recent food tour of the area. It's one of those food memories where if I close my eyes tightly and count to three, I am transported back to the cookery class. I can almost smell the aroma of the freshly grated nutmeg whilst hearing Nonna Violante explain everything with such precision. *Passatelli* are not only simple to make and an absolute joy to eat, they are frugal, using basic ingredients – in essence *cucina povera* cooking, in my opinion the best way to cook and eat.

————

Preparation time 1 hour
Cooking time 5 minutes
Serves 4

————

300g stale breadcrumbs
200g Parmesan, grated
4 medium eggs
Zest of ½ lemon
1 tsp nutmeg, freshly grated
Pinch of salt
3 litres, chicken stock
50g '00' flour (if required)

1 Onto a wooden board, place the breadcrumbs and Parmesan. Stir with your hands to combine and make a well in the centre.
2 Crack the eggs into the centre of the well.
3 Add the lemon zest, nutmeg and pinch of salt.
4 Using a fork, slowly work the eggs around to incorporate the breadcrumb mixture. Work the eggs into a dough and knead for 3 minutes. If the dough is a little wet add a little '00' flour to bring the dough together.
5 Cover the dough in cling film and allow to rest for a minimum of 10 minutes.
6 Place the chicken stock on to boil whilst you prepare the *passatelli* pasta.
7 Cut the dough into small workable sections.
8 Press each section of dough through a traditional *passatelli* press or use a potato ricer with holes that should be 5mm in diameter (larger than a standard potato ricer).
9 Pass the *passatelli* through the press and cut them with a sharp knife when they are 4cm in length. Lay them gently onto a tea towel and continue until you have used all of the prepared dough.
10 Cook the *passatelli* in the stock for around 3 minutes. Ladle into bowls, scatter with additional Parmesan and fall in love.

CARMELA'S TIPS
When making *passatelli* it is essential that the breadcrumbs are stale and the bread contains no olive oil as this will affect the cooking of the *passatelli*, making them fall apart. Many chefs also add a little '00' flour to their *passatelli* dough to help it combine. Feel free to do this but be aware it's considered cheating!

PASTA DUMPLINGS WITH BORLOTTI BEANS

PISAREI E FASO

There is an old wives' tale attached to this pasta shape. Due to the shape, the thumb is used to apply pressure to the dough forming a dent, hence possibly leaving a tough outer skin on the thumb if they were made often enough. If a well-used thumb was seen on a young lady then is was said she would make a perfect wife and mother. *Pisarei* (pasta dumplings) are still made by grandmothers, mothers and daughters and are from the province of Piacenza in Emilia-Romagna. The art of making pasta is still very much loved in Italy, especially within the family home, and I like the idea of the fairy tale too, which adds a sense of romance.

———————

Preparation time 1 hour
Cooking time 30 minutes
Serves 4

———————

FOR THE PASTA
400g '00' flour
150g stale white breadcrumbs
350ml–380ml warm water

FOR THE SAUCE
1 tbsp olive oil
50g unsalted butter
1 medium onion, peeled and
    finely chopped
30g *strutto* or lard
2 garlic cloves, peeled and crushed
Small bunch of parsley, chopped
600g passata
100ml water
1 tbsp tomato purée
1 x 400g tin borlotti beans, drained
Salt and pepper to season
10 basil leaves, torn
70g Parmesan, grated

CARMELA'S TIPS
If you prefer, you can soak beans the day before and cook them for much longer. I cheat by using canned as they take a lot of the initial preparation out of cooking. Borlotti beans can be replaced with cannellini beans, butter beans or chickpeas.

———————

1 Into a bowl, tumble in the flour and breadcrumbs and stir.

2 Make a well in the centre and slowly add the water.

3 Form the mixture into a ball of dough using your hands.

4 Knead for 4 minutes on a lightly floured surface until elastic and smooth. Cover and allow to rest for 30 minutes.

5 Once rested, cut the dough into four portions. Roll each quarter out into thin sausages. Using a knife, cut each into small pieces of dough. The pasta should not be too thick and should be the size of a swollen borlotti bean. Use your thumb to push each small piece and make a concave dent.

6 Continue making the pasta in this way. Place each dumpling onto a clean tea towel to dry a little whilst you make the sauce.

7 Into a shallow saucepan, add the olive oil, butter and onion. Fry off the onion for 2 minutes over a low heat until softened.

8 Add the *strutto* or lard, garlic and parsley. Stir well.

9 Pour in the passata along with the water, tomato purée and drained borlotti beans. Stir and season with salt and pepper. Cook slowly for 30 minutes.

10 Cook the *pisarei* in salted water until *al dente*. Drain, reserving a small ladle of the starchy pasta water.

11 Add the pasta and reserved water to the sauce and stir gently. Add the basil leaves.

12 Serve in bowls with some grated Parmesan.

TORTELLINI IN STOCK
TORTELLINI CON BRODO

Emilia-Romagna is at the heart of pasta; the region has to be one of the most deliciously rich I have ever visited. I just wish I could include more than five recipes per region. The pasta is superb and the range vast. Here I use tiny *tortellini*, which resemble little belly buttons. You could equally make them a little larger and they would be called *tortelloni*. I advise you to make the filling the day before, not only to save time but also to allow the flavours to develop.

Preparation time 1 hour 40 minutes
Cooking time 20 minutes
Serves 4

FOR THE PASTA
400g prepared egg pasta dough (page 13)
Polenta, for dusting

FOR THE FILLING
25g unsalted butter
1 tbsp olive oil
100g pork shoulder (boned and minced)
50ml white wine
100g mortadella
100g Parma ham
100g Parmesan, grated (plus extra
    for the table)
1 large egg
Salt and pepper to season
Pinch of freshly grated nutmeg

FOR THE STOCK
2 litres chicken stock

1 In a frying pan, heat the butter and olive oil. Add the pork and fry off on a medium heat. Once browned all over, add the white wine and allow to evaporate. When the mince is cooked through, remove from the heat.
2 Place the mince, mortadella, Parma ham, Parmesan and egg into a food processor. Blitz for 30 seconds.
3 Spoon into a bowl. Season with salt, pepper and some freshly grated nutmeg. Cover and pop in the fridge until required.
4 Roll the pasta dough out either with a pasta machine as described on page 13 or using a rolling pin. I prefer to roll out the dough for tortellini using my metre-long rolling pin. You are looking for a perfectly thin and smooth *sfoglia* (sheet); the ideal thickness would be that of a *scopa* (playing card). Once you have a sheet of pasta, cut the dough into 5cm x 5cm squares.
5 Put a teaspoon of filling onto the centre of each tortellini square. Seal with a little water, forming the pasta into a triangle.
6 Hold the triangle in your hand with the tip pointing upwards.
7 Encourage the edges of the dough upwards and attach both lower corners together.
8 Repeat and place the *tortellini* onto a tray dusted with polenta to dry off slightly.
9 Place the pan of stock on to boil. Once boiling, gently add the *tortellini*. They will take about 3 minutes or so to cook.
10 Cook until *al dente*. Ladle the *tortellini* and stock into warm bowls and garnish with a finishing flurry of grated Parmesan.

CARMELA'S TIPS
Alternative fillings include a simple spinach, ricotta, Parmesan and nutmeg, or roasted squash or pumpkin with a smooth mascarpone and Parmesan.

FRIULI-VENEZIA GIULIA

Friuli-Venezia Giulia is situated in the northeast of Italy bordering Veneto, Austria, Slovenia and the Adriatic Sea. A region rich and diverse in culture, it encompasses a wide variety of dishes taking influences from its Venetian neighbour and European borders.

The region is in essence split into two: Friuli, the slightly poorer side of the region, and Venezia Giulia, which is incredibly prosperous. Trieste is the capital.

Pork, veal, lamb, goat and freshwater fish such as pike, eel, trout and tench are abundant in this region. In the most northwest part of the region *prosciutto di San Daniele*, a beautiful leg of pork, using only pigs bred and fed in Italy, is produced in the province of Udine. This region has a wonder of pasta dishes to offer too, even though pasta isn't at the forefront of the kitchen table. That said, the dishes that are included in this chapter are simply mouth-watering. My favourites are a rolled spinach and ricotta-filled *strucolo* baked pasta dish and another made with freshly ground sugar and poppy seed sprinkled over fresh egg pasta. The regional speciality are *cjalsons*, a kind of dumpling made from potato pasta dough, rolled and filled with sweet and savoury mixtures

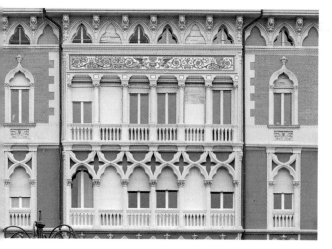

▲ The facade of an Art Noveau Palace in Trieste, the wealthy capital of the region.

▶ View from Arcano Castle near Udine, in Fruili-Venezia Guilia.

AUBERGINE FILLED RAVIOLI WITH A SIMPLE TOMATO SAUCE

BAULETTI DI PASTA CON CREMA DI MELANZANE

Bauletto translates as 'travelling case', so I make these ravioli into rectangular parcels and pack them with my desired filling. To be honest, any filled pasta shape would work well here. Made from a dough that combines flours from the north and south of Italy and filled with the essence, aroma and flavour of the Mediterranean, they're absolutely delicious.

Preparation time 1 hour
Cooking time 20 minutes
Serves 4

FOR THE PASTA DOUGH
300g semolina flour
 (*semola di grano duro*)
100g '00' flour
4 large eggs

FOR THE FILLING
2 medium aubergines
2 whole garlic cloves, skins on
1 tbsp ground almonds
30g Parmesan, grated
Salt and pepper to season

FOR THE SAUCE (SUGO)
1 tbsp olive oil
1 garlic clove, peeled and thinly sliced
1 x 400g tin chopped tomatoes
10 basil leaves, roughly torn
Salt and pepper to season
Extra virgin olive oil to finish
80g Parmesan, grated

1 Combine the pasta flours and tumble onto a wooden board. Make a well in the centre of the flour and crack in the eggs. Use a fork to whisk the eggs and gently combine the flour fully.

2 Form into a ball and knead for 5 minutes until smooth and elastic. Cover with cling film and allow to rest for 30 minutes at room temperature.

3 Preheat the oven to 190°C (gas 5).

4 Take the aubergines and pierce them all over with a fork.

5 Place the aubergines on a wire rack in the oven and bake for 30 minutes. Ten minutes before the aubergines are ready, place the garlic cloves onto a little foil and bake alongside the aubergine.

6 Once the aubergines are tender remove them from the oven along with the sweet garlic.

7 Peel the aubergines and place the pulp in a bowl along with the roasted garlic.

8 Sprinkle in the almonds and 30g Parmesan along with a twist of salt and pepper. Stir well and set aside.

9 To make the sauce, pour the olive oil into a shallow saucepan and add the sliced garlic. Fry gently over a medium heat for 3 minutes.

10 Add the tinned tomatoes and basil and season with salt and pepper. Cook for 25 minutes while you prepare the pasta.

11 Cut the dough in half, cover one half with cling film and roll the other portion of pasta dough out using a rolling pin or pasta machine if preferred.

12 Roll the dough into two long rectangular sheets.

13 Place the pasta filling into a disposable piping bag and secure the top.

14 Onto one sheet of pasta, pipe 5cm lengths of filling intermittently across the length of the dough, then repeat below if space allows.

15 Place the other pasta sheet on top and secure around the fillings, using your hands to cup the dough around the filling and remove any excess air.

16 Using a pastry roller, cut in between each ravioli and set aside. Repeat with the set aside pasta dough, until all of the mixture has been used.

17 Place a large pan of water on to boil. Once boiling, salt well and add the ravioli. Cook until *al dente*.

18 Drain the pasta and add the parcels to the sauce in the pan. Serve with a drizzle of olive oil and an additional sprinkle of Parmesan.

BUCKWHEAT MALTAGLIATI PASTA WITH BROWNED BUTTER AND PARMESAN

BLECS

The love of grains is shown within many pasta recipes from this particular region. I always find that when you add buckwheat to a pasta dish it becomes robust and somehow comforting. *Maltagliati* pasta in essence is badly cut pasta, a little misshapen. All of the pasta *sfoglia* (sheet) is used by cutting rough pieces of dough in more or less the same shape and size. The simplicity of this dish makes it a lovely warming lunch. It you like a somewhat nutty and textured polenta topping, then this recipe is for you.

Preparation time 1 hour
Cooking time 10 minutes
Serves 4

FOR THE PASTA DOUGH
250g '00' flour
250g buckwheat flour
4 large eggs

FOR THE SAUCE
155g unsalted butter
110g polenta
A few parsley leaves, roughly chopped
70g Montasio (regional cheese) or
    Parmesan, grated

1 Combine the '00' and buckwheat flours. Tumble the flour onto a wooden board, make a well in the centre and crack in the eggs.
2 Using a fork (or fingertips if preferred), combine the eggs with the flour. Knead for 5 minutes until smooth and elastic. Wrap in cling film and leave the dough to rest at room temperature for 30 minutes.
3 Roll out the dough with a rolling pin to the thickness of a 10p piece. Use a fluted pastry wheel to cut similar-sized pieces of small triangular pasta.
4 Allow the freshly cut pasta to rest for 30 minutes.
5 Place a large pan of water on to boil. Once boiling, salt well, add the pasta and cook until *al dente*.
6 In a small pan, melt the butter and over a medium heat for 4 minutes. Pour in the polenta and stir. Cook until the polenta turns a nutty colour, 3 minutes or so.
7 Drain the pasta and add to the nutty sauce. Stir in the parsley and half the grated cheese.
8 Serve in warm bowls with an additional sprinkle of cheese.

LASAGNE SHEETS WITH MELTED BUTTER, SUGAR AND POPPY SEEDS

LASAGNA AL PAPAVERO

This pasta dish hails from beautiful Trieste. Trieste is situated in the northern-most point of Italy on the border with Slovenia. Simple pasta sheets but with a hint of naughtiness, this dish is honestly sensational. The light texture of poppy seeds with the sweetness of sugar is the perfect pairing. I often have pasta with a sprinkle of sugar as a pick-me-up, the carbs and sugar work so well.

Preparation time 1 hour
Cooking time 10 minutes
Serves 4

400g fresh egg pasta dough (page 13)
50g poppy seeds
2 tbsp sugar
120g unsalted butter

1 Roll the pasta dough out to the thickness of a 10p piece or until you can see your hands through it.

2 Cut the dough into 10cm x 4cm pieces. Allow to dry for 15 minutes.

3 Into a pestle and mortar, add the poppy seeds and sugar. Combine and grind for one minute.

4 Place a large pan of water on to boil. Once boiling, salt well, add the pasta and cook until *al dente*.

5 Melt the butter in a small frying pan until just browned.

6 Drain the pasta and return to the pan.

7 Add the melted butter and toss.

8 Serve the pasta with a sprinkle of the poppy seed and sugar blend.

PASTA SPINACH ROULADE

STRUCOLO DA SINAZE

Out of all the pasta recipes in my books, my favourites have to be filled pasta dishes – from a regional lasagne from Molise to the delicious *vincisgrassi* from Le Marche. With this *strucolo* I have used a fresh egg pasta dough, but it can be made with a potato-based pasta dough too. I think the easiest way to cook this dish is in a fish kettle purely for reasons of space and comfort. This dish is also known as *rotolo* in Emilia-Romagna.

———

Preparation time 1 hour
Cooking time 45 minutes
Serves 6

———

500g fresh egg pasta dough (page 13)

FOR THE PASTA FILLING
500g ricotta
600g spinach, blanched
100g Grana Padano, grated
1 egg yolk
½ tsp freshly grated nutmeg
Small bunch of basil, roughly torn
Salt and pepper to season

FOR THE SAUCE (SUGO)
3 tbsp olive oil
1 garlic clove, peeled and finely crushed
600g passata
Bunch of basil leaves, roughly torn
Pinch of dried oregano
Salt and pepper to season

1 To make the filling, place the ricotta in a large bowl and use a wooden spoon to break it up a little.

2 Ensure the blanched spinach has been squeezed very well to eliminate excess moisture. Chop the spinach and combine with the ricotta.

3 Add the Grana Padano, egg yolk, nutmeg and basil to the ricotta mixture, season and stir well. Cover with cling film and chill whilst you prepare the pasta dough.

4 Roll the pasta dough out with a rolling pin to the thickness of a 50p piece, approximately 40cm long and 25cm wide.

5 Place the pasta sheet onto a piece of cling film that's lying on top of a piece of muslin slightly bigger than the *strucolo* pasta dough.

6 Spread the ricotta mixture all over the pasta dough sheet, leaving a 1cm gap all the way round.

7 Lift the cling film and use it to help you roll the pasta into a sausage.

8 Roll the cling film tightly around the *strucolo*, secure and twist the ends like a sweet.

9 Roll the muslin around the cling-filmed *strucolo* and secure firmly with ties.

10 Lay the *strucolo* in the fish kettle and fill it with water. Salt well and gently boil the pasta for 30 minutes.

11 To make the sugo, pour the olive oil to a small sauté pan, add the garlic and fry over a low heat for 1 minute.

12 Add the passata, basil and oregano. Stir and cook for 25 minutes. Season with salt and pepper.

13 Preheat the oven to 190°C (gas 5)

14 Once the pasta is cooked, remove from the heat, allow to cool for 15 minutes and then unwrap. Spoon half the sauce into the base of an ovenware dish. Slice the *strucolo* into 3cm discs and place on top of the sauce.

15 Spoon the remaining tomato sauce on top of the *strucolo* and sprinkle over some freshly grated Grana Padano. Bake for 15 minutes.

16 Serve on warmed plates.

SWEET AND SOUR FILLED POTATO PASTA

CJALSONS, CJALZON

There are so many variations to this dish, along with many names and spellings. *Cjalsons* consist of a potato-based pasta dough with a sweet and sour filling, a great dish to experiment with when it comes to fillings. Persevere, as the potato can make the dough a little tricky to roll and work with, but it's worth the effort.

———

Preparation time 1 hour
Cooking time 30 minutes
Serves 4

———

FOR THE PASTA DOUGH
300g potatoes (Maris piper), unpeeled
280g '00' flour
1 egg yolk
Pinch of salt

FOR THE FILLING
1 tbsp olive oil
1 small onion, peeled and finely chopped
2 medium potatoes
Mixed fresh herbs (parsley, fennel, mint, thyme, basil), roughly chopped
1 small apple, peeled and grated
1 small pear, peeled and grated
Zest of 1 lemon
3 amaretti biscuits, crushed
1 tbsp apricot jam
30g chocolate, melted
½ tsp cinnamon
20g unsalted butter, melted
Salt to season

FOR THE TOPPING
70g butter
50g *ricotta salata*

1 Bring a pan of water to the boil and cook the potatoes with their skins on until tender.

2 Drain, cool and peel. Push the potatoes through a ricer and place them into a large mixing bowl along with the flour, egg yolk and pinch of salt. Combine and tumble onto a board. Knead for one minute (do not overwork), cover and allow to rest for 30 minutes while you prepare the filling.

3 In a frying pan, heat the oil and fry off the onion for 5 minutes.

4 Add the riced potatoes and stir. Cook for an additional minute then spoon the mixture into a clean bowl.

5 Sprinkle in the chopped herbs, apple, pear, lemon zest, amaretti, apricot jam, chocolate, cinnamon, butter and twist of salt.

6 Stir well to combine this mixture fully.

7 Roll the pasta dough out to the thickness of a 50p coin. Cut out discs of pasta 10cm in diameter.

8 Spoon a heaped teaspoon of the filling onto the centre of each disc, fold into a half moon and seal. Repeat with the remaining pasta dough and filling.

9 Place a large pan of water on to boil. Once boiling, salt well, add the pasta and cook for 5 minutes.

10 To make a topping, melt the butter in a small frying pan and cook for 5 minutes until slightly browned.

11 Drain the pasta, spoon into warmed bowls and drizzle over a little butter and grated *ricotta salate*.

LAZIO

In the centre of Italy, holding Rome firmly as its capital, Lazio borders so many regions – Tuscany, Campania and Abruzzo, to name a few. What a region this is. Rome is full of many underground secrets and bursting with dreams and romance for so many. I have visited the city a few times now and I fall a little more in love with its splendour every time.

So what wonders we will find in this delicious region? I have included five recipes, all using a long pasta shape. Just remember the wonderful quote from Sophia Loren: 'Everything you see I owe to spaghetti', an apt quote for this region. Spaghetti carbonara: long delicate strands of spaghetti with *guanciale*, egg yolks and Parmesan. No cream is necessary at all and the combination of (free-range) egg yolks and Parmesan stirred ferociously, combined with hot pasta and smoky *guanciale* (cured pork cheek) makes for the most delicious bowl of pasta. You can also add a little of the starchy pasta water to emulsify the sauce a little more. These are simple classic dishes made with speed and to be enjoyed around your family table any day of the week.

▲ Strips of the very spicy *coppiette*, a culinary specialty of Lazio.

▶ The medieval hilltop town of Bagnoreggio in Lazio.

BUCATINI WITH CHEESE AND PEPPER
BUCATINI CACIO E PEPE

This recipes fills me with joy. Three of the very best ingredients, *bucatini*, Pecorino Romano and coarse ground black pepper make for one of the most iconic dishes to have come out of Italy. It's simple *cucina povera* cooking; however, this recipe is not from the south of Italy but from Rome. A dish that offers no hiding places at all for poor quality ingredients, use the very best produce, and if no one's watching add a light drizzle of extra virgin olive oil to finish.

———

Preparation time 2 minutes
Cooking time 10 minutes
Serves 4

———

400g *bucatini*
90g Pecorino Romano, grated
  (plus extra for the table)
Freshly ground black pepper
Extra virgin olive oil, to drizzle

1 Place a large pan of water on to boil. Once boiling, salt well with coarse salt.
2 Add the *bucatini* and cook until *al dente*. Drain and reserve 220ml of the pasta water.
3 Place the *bucatini* back into the saucepan, along with the grated pecorino and reserved pasta water. Stir well off the heat to emulsify.
4 Add a generous grind of black pepper, stir and serve in warm bowls with an additional scattering of pecorino.

CARMELA'S TIPS
Break the three-ingredient rule and add a little drizzle of extra virgin olive oil and some chopped fresh herbs. You can also lightly dry roast the the black pepper and grind.

———

BUCATINI WITH TOMATOES AND GUANCIALE

BUCATINI ALL' AMATRICIANA

Is this pasta dish called *matriciana* or *amatriciana* and does it belong to Lazio or Abruzzo? This is still causing arguments around many a regional kitchen table, I'll let you decide. My thoughts are *bucatini all' amatriciana* is named after the town of Amatrice, in the province of Rieti, just over an hour east of Rome. Long leggy *bucatini* loves a robust sauce. It is a thick spaghetti with a hole or *bucco* that runs right along the centre of each strand. This dish oozes with a subtle spiciness and a great depth of flavour that comes from the salty *guanciale* pork cheeks.

Preparation time 20 minutes
Cooking time 30 minutes
Serves 4

400g *bucatini*
3 tbsp olive oil
1 small onion, peeled and diced
400g *guanciale*, diced
1 garlic clove, peeled and crushed
4 large tomatoes, peeled and sliced
1 small chilli, deseeded and
  finely chopped
Small bunch of basil, torn
90g Pecorino Romano, grated
  (plus extra for the table)

1 Place a large pan of water on to boil in preparation for cooking the *bucatini*.

2 Pour the olive oil into a frying pan and add the diced onion. Cook for 5 minutes then add the *guanciale*.

3 Stir and cook until the *guanciale* is lightly coloured all over. Add the garlic and stir.

4 To the pan add the tomatoes and chilli and season with salt and pepper.

5 Once the pasta water is bubbling, salt well, stir and add the *bucatini*. Cook per packet instructions, minus 2 minutes to ensure the pasta remains *al dente*.

6 Drain the *bucatini*, reserving 80ml of pasta water, and add the pasta directly to the sauce. Turn up the heat for 2 minutes, stir and add the pasta water. Scatter over the torn basil and combine.

7 Add half the pecorino and stir.

8 Serve the *bucatini* in bowls scattered over with some extra pecorino.

CARMELA'S TIPS
Spaghetti can be used instead of *bucatini*, as can tinned San Marzano tomatoes in place of fresh.

SPAGHETTI CARBONARA

SPAGHETTI ALLA CARBONARA

This is a light spaghetti carbonara from the region of Lazio, said to have been created in Rome just after World War ll. The history, in my opinion, is still a little uncertain. Is the dish named after the coalminers *(carbonari)*, has it been part of the Italian food scene for many years, or did the Americans bring it over just after World War II? All I know is that I adore this dish for its simplicity. Just remember *senza panna* ('without cream') – *never ever* make carbonara with cream.

Preparation time 5 minutes
Cooking time 12 minutes
Serves 4

400g dried spaghetti
1 tsp olive oil
450g *guanciale* (cured pork cheek) or
   pancetta, cubed
100g Pecorino Romano, grated
   (plus a little extra for topping)
1 large egg plus 5 large egg yolks
Salt and pepper to season
1 tbsp chopped parsley
1 tbsp chopped basil

1 Cook the spaghetti according to the packet instructions in salted boiling water, minus 2 minutes to ensure it remains *al dente*.
2 Heat the olive oil in a frying pan and cook the *guanciale* for 5 minutes until lightly golden.
3 In a bowl, mix together the pecorino, whole egg and yolks, season with salt and pepper and add the chopped parsley. Reserve 20g of the pecorino for serving
4 Drain the spaghetti (reserving 70ml of pasta water) and add the pasta to the *guanciale*, stir well. Stir the egg sauce into the spaghetti and pour in the reserved pasta water. This will help to emulsify the sauce and the heat of the pancetta and spaghetti will cook the egg mixture as you stir. Sprinkle in the chopped basil.
5 Serve in large bowls with the reserved grated pecorino sprinkled over the top

CARMELA'S TIPS
Try making *Spaghetti alla griscia*
too. This is in essence the same as a
carbonara, but you simply omit the eggs.

SEAFOOD CARBONARA
CARBONARA DI MARE

This recipe is a deliciously light alternative to the traditional pancetta or *guanciale*-based carbonara. In this seafood version you can use more or less any fish and seafood that takes your fancy. Try something a little different that's in season. Here I have included small prawns for added texture and flavour; clams would work equally well, the sweet jewels of the Mediterranean.

————

Preparation time 20 minutes
Cooking time 15 minutes
Serves 4

————

400g dried spaghetti
150g swordfish
100g salmon
60g fresh tuna
2 sprigs of fresh thyme
15 prawns, cleaned and shells removed
3 egg yolks
1 whole large egg
60g Pecorino Romano, grated
Salt and pepper to season
3 tbsp olive oil
Small handful of parsley, chopped

1 Cube the swordfish, salmon, and tuna into 2cm x 2cm pieces.
2 Put a large pan of water on to boil. Salt well, add the spaghetti and cook according to the packet instructions, minus 2 minutes so the pasta remains *al dente*.
3 In a bowl, add the egg yolks, whole egg, Parmesan and a pinch of salt and pepper. Whisk to combine and set aside.
4 Fry off the fish and prawns in a little olive oil with a few sprigs of thyme. This will take about 6 minutes. Season with a pinch of salt and pepper.
5 Drain the spaghetti, reserving about 30ml of the water.
6 Return the spaghetti to the pan and add the cooked fish, egg mixture and reserved pasta water.
7 Mix really well until the spaghetti is well coated and the sauce has become creamy.
8 Serve in warm bowls with a scattering of chopped parsley.

THE POPE'S FETTUCCINE

FETTUCCINE ALLA PAPALINA

This fettuccine is not what you would expect from the region of Lazio. Butter and cream (traditionally used in the northern regions) are used to make a delicious sauce that was enjoyed by cardinals from the Vatican in a Roman *trattoria* many years ago. The dish was named after Pope Pio XII, who tasted it and loved the richness. Similar to a carbonara but with a twist, it's made with fettuccine, a long pasta which is slightly wider and a little thicker than the very well-known tagliatelle.

Preparation time 10 minutes
Cooking time 20 minutes
Serves 4

400g fettuccine
50g unsalted butter
1 tbsp olive oil
1 small shallot, peeled and finely
    chopped
150g *prosciutto crudo* (Parma ham)
    sliced into strips
200ml double cream
2 large whole eggs, plus 2 yolks
80g Pecorino Romano, grated
    (plus extra for the table)
Salt and pepper to season
200g peas (from the freezer)
2 tbsp parsley, chopped

1 Place a large pan of water on to boil. Once boiled, salt well.
2 Add the butter and olive oil to a large sauté pan. Over a low heat, add the shallots and *prosciutto crudo* and cook gently without colouring. Cook the shallots until they are translucent in colour, around 5 minutes.
3 Pour in the cream, stir and remove from the heat.
4 Into a small bowl, crack in the eggs, add the additional yolks and Pecorino Romano and season with salt and black pepper.
5 Cook the *fettuccine* and peas together in the boiling water.
6 Once the *fettuccine* is *al dente*, drain (reserving 70ml of the pasta water)
7 Place the cream mixture on a very low heat and tumble in the *fettuccine* and peas. Stir to coat every strand, then pour in the egg mixture and a little of the reserved pasta water.
8 Remove from the heat to avoid scrambling and stir well to combine. Add enough pasta water to help emulsify the sauce.
9 Sprinkle on the chopped parsley and serve with an additional sprinkle of pecorino, if desired.

LE MARCHE

A hidden gem stretching 100 miles along the Adriatic coast on the eastern side of Italy, the region of Le Marche borders Emilia-Romagna, Tuscany, Umbria, Abruzzo and Lazio. Beautiful beaches, rocking fishing boats and stunning coastal views offer wonderful family holidays, while further inland, the land is much hillier, providing the perfect terrain for farmers and shepherds. Ancona is the capital city of this region and it sits in an attractive, very busy seaport.

▲ Flowering onion field in Le Marche.

▶ The Duomo in Urbino, Le Marche.

The food of the region is a combination of fresh seasonal fruit and vegetables along with freshly caught fish, specialist pork, lamb, rabbit and goat. This region showcases the simplicity of *cucina povera* cooking of the south along with the richer flavours of the north. Le Marche's famous pasta dish is *vincigrassi*, a rich and somewhat unique lasagne layered with livers, sweetbreads and chicken. I love this dish. Not only for its filling but because of the pasta dough, made with a light touch of butter and a kiss of Marsala. What more can I say? Welcome to Le Marche.

MEZZALUNE WITH SOLE AND SHELLFISH
RAVIOLI AI FILETTE DI SOGLIOLA CON LE COZZE E VONGOLE

With this recipe we are taking our inspiration from the coast and I have opted for half-moon parcels of pasta known as *mezzalune*. You could of course make a standard round or square ravioli if preferred. Use fish that is easily accessible to you. I adore red mullet but it's often a little tricky to come by without pre-ordering.

Preparation time 1 hour
Cooking time 15 minutes
Serves 4

400g freshly prepared egg pasta dough
  (page 13)
Polenta, for dusting

FOR THE RAVIOLI FILLING
2 tbsp olive oil
1 garlic clove, peeled and finely sliced
Small bunch of parsley, finely chopped
10 basil leaves, roughly chopped
100g sole fillets, skin and bones
  removed, portioned
100g sea bass or bream fillets, skin and
  bones removed, portioned
125ml white wine or vermouth
1 large baked potato, peeled
Salt and pepper to season

FOR THE SEAFOOD SAUCE
3 tbsp olive oil
2 garlic cloves, peeled and finely sliced
350g cherry or baby plum tomatoes,
  quartered
250g mussels
250g clams
150ml white wine (or vermouth
  is a good alternative)
Handful of celery leaves, finely sliced
1 small fresh red chilli, deseeded and
  finely sliced
Salt and pepper to season
Small bunch of basil, torn

1 Start by preparing the pasta filling. This can be prepared a day ahead if preferred. Pour the olive oil into a shallow pan and add the garlic, parsley and basil. Stir and cook over a low heat for 3 minutes.
2 Add the fish fillets and stir. Cook for 5 minutes over a medium heat then add the white wine or vermouth.
3 Cook the fish for 5 minutes; this will allow the wine to evaporate.
4 Into a food processor, add the baked potato and cooked fish. Blitz until smooth, taste and season with a twist of salt and pepper.
5 Spoon the mixture into a disposable piping bag and set aside.
6 Roll out the prepared egg pasta as described on page 13.
7 Using a 7cm circular cutter, cut out discs of pasta.
8 Take the piping bag and pipe a teaspoonful-sized mound of filling onto each circle.
9 Take the circle in your hand and fold the dough in half, removing any trapped air. Secure so you have a half moon shape. Continue with the remaining pasta and filling.
10 Once the *mezzalune* are all made, place onto a clean tea towel or a tray dusted with polenta.
11 Place a large pan of water on to boil for the pasta and once boiling, salt well.
12 To make the sauce, pour the oil into a large shallow sauté pan and add the garlic. Cook over a medium heat for 2 minutes.
13 Tumble in the cherry tomatoes and stir. Cook for an additional 5 minutes.
14 Meanwhile, cook the pasta over a low heat for 4 minutes until *al dente*.
15 Add the mussels, clams and white wine to the tomatoes. Clamp on a lid and cook for a few minutes until the shellfish are all fully opened.
16 Add the celery leaves, chilli and a pinch of salt and pepper to season.
17 Use a slotted spoon to remove the ravioli from the water and into the seafood sauce. Lightly combine, add the remaining basil and serve.

PASSATELLI IN STOCK WITH BONE MARROW

PASSATELLI IN BRODO

It seems that not only the region of Romagna hails the wonderful *passatelli*. This style of *cucina povera* cooking is also very much loved and embraced with open arms in Le Marche. If you have time, make a simple chicken stock, using either the carcas or pieces of chicken along with the giblets and a basic *soffritto* (carrot, celery and onion, diced). If I serve *passatelli* with seafood I tend to increase the lemon zest for freshness, whereas when I serve it with stock I reduce it slightly.

Preparation time 1 hour
Cooking time 15 minutes
Serves 4

150g spinach, blanched
5 medium eggs
600g breadcrumbs
400g Parmesan, grated (plus extra for the table)
½ tsp freshly grated nutmeg
Zest of 1 small lemon
Salt and pepper to season
20g bone marrow, worked into a paste (use melted butter if preferred)
70g '00' flour (if required)
2 litres of chicken or beef stock

1 Into a food processor, add the blanched spinach and eggs. Blitz for 30 seconds until you have a smooth yet textured mixture.
2 Tumble the breadcrumbs and Parmesan onto a wooden board, mix to combine. Sprinkle over the nutmeg and lemon zest.
3 Season with a little twist of salt and black pepper.
4 Make a well in the centre of the dry ingredients and add the bone marrow and spinach mixture. Use a fork to slowly combine, working from the inside, out.
5 Form the mixture into a dough and knead for 2 minutes. If the mixture is a little wet add some '00' flour. Wrap with cling film and set aside for 15 minutes.
6 Cut the dough into workable portions. Cut in half and press through a *passatelli* press or wide-holed potato ricer to pieces the length of 5cm.
7 Place the stock on to simmer. Cook the *passatelli* in the stock for around 3–5 minutes until they float to the top of the pan.
8 Ladle into warm bowls with an additional sprinkle of Parmesan.

CARMELA'S TIPS
Passatelli should be treated with care as they are very delicate. I love them served with baby roasted tomatoes and also seafood. Please note the spinach in this recipe does make the *passatelli* dough very wet, so please have some '00' flour to hand and use as required.

SPAGHETTI WITH PORCINI AND VEAL

SPAGHETTI ALLA CHITARRA CON PORCINI

Hopping over into the border from Abruzzo into Le Marche armed with my wooden strung 'chitarra' pasta press, I bring the delicate spaghetti known as *alla chitarra*. These delicate strands can take on most sauces. Here I have opted for an autumnal veal and woodland porcini mix, two of my favourite ingredients.

———

Preparation time 50 minutes
Cooking time 1 hour 30 minutes
Serves 4

———

400g prepared spaghetti *alla chitarra* (page 50) or dried
100ml boiling water
25g porcini mushrooms
3 tbsp olive oil
1 shallot, peeled and finely sliced
1 garlic clove, peeled and crushed
300g veal mince
50ml red wine
2 tbsp tomato purée
5 sprigs of thyme, plus extra to finish
250ml chicken stock
Salt and pepper to season
80g Parmesan, grated (optional)

1 Pour the boiling water into a small bowl and soak the porcini mushrooms for at least 20 minutes.

2 Pour the olive oil into a large shallow sauté pan and add the sliced shallot and garlic. Fry gently over a medium heat for 5 minutes.

3 Tumble the veal mince into the shallots and stir, breaking up any larger pieces with the back of a wooden spoon. Cook until coloured all over.

4 Pour in the red wine and tomato purée and add the thyme sprigs. Stir well.

5 Spoon the softened porcini mushrooms into the veal and stir.

6 Drain the porcini water through a sieve with tiny holes or a piece of muslin to collect any tiny amounts of grit. Add the porcini water to the sauce and stir.

7 Spoon in half the chicken stock and stir.

8 Season with salt and pepper. Simmer over a medium heat for 1 hour 15 minutes. Halfway through cooking, add the remaining chicken stock and stir.

9 Place a large pan of water on to boil. Once boiling, salt well and cook the spaghetti until *al dente*.

10 Drain the spaghetti then add the pasta to the sauce and stir.

11 Serve in warm bowls with a sprinkle of Parmesan, if desired, and a scattering of fresh delicate thyme leaves.

CARMELA'S TIPS
Tagliatelle (pictured here) works very well with this sauce, too. My local Italian shop now stock dried *spaghetti alla chitarra*.

———

TAGLIOLINI FROM CAMPOFILONE WITH SMOKED PANCETTA

MACCHERONCINI DI CAMPOFILONE CON PANCETTA

Campofilone in Le Marche still boasts some very beautifully made egg pasta. The pasta factory replicates pasta just as Nonna would make it, so this dish hails from that small town. The fact that Italy still embraces its traditions and has such pride in its pasta means my obsession continues to bloom.

────────

Preparation time 10 minutes
Cooking time 30 minutes
Serves 4

────────

400g *tagliolini*
2 tbsp olive oil
1 shallot, peeled and finely sliced
1 garlic clove, peeled and crushed
25g lard (*strutto*)
250g pancetta, smoked
1 small chilli, deseeded and finely
    chopped
70ml white wine
50ml double cream
1 tbsp tomato purée
1 x 680g bottle passata
Salt and pepper to season
Small bunch fresh basil, roughly torn
80g Parmesan, grated

1 Pour the olive oil into a shallow pan and fry off the shallot and garlic for 3 minutes.
2 Add the lard and pancetta. Stir with a wooden spoon and cook for 10 minutes until the pancetta is golden all over.
3 Sprinkle in the chilli and white wine. Stir and cook for 5 minutes.
4 Pour in the cream and stir, followed by the tomato purée and passata.
5 Season with salt and pepper and add half the basil. Cook for 25 minutes.
6 Place a large pan of water on to boil for the pasta and once boiling, salt well.
7 Cook the *tagliolini* until *al dente* (with resistance and bite). Drain the pasta.
8 Combine the sauce with the pasta, add the remaining basil and half the Parmesan, combine fully and serve with an additional sprinkling of Parmesan.

VINCIGRASSI LASAGNE

VINCIGRASSI

If you ask anyone from Le Marche what they consider their signature pasta dish, I'm sure *vincigrassi* would be at the top of the list. A typical lasagne dish from Le Marche, it features no tomatoes but layers of pasta filled with mushrooms, chicken, chicken livers and truffle, wrapped in a béchamel sauce. If you wanted to make lasagne then this version would most definitely be a celebration dish. Time must be on your side but the finished dish is something well worthy of a central role on any family table.

Preparation time 1 hour 30 minutes
Cooking time 45–60 minutes
Serves 6

FOR THE PASTA DOUGH
150g semolina flour
    (*semola di grano duro*)
300g '00' flour
30g unsalted butter, melted
3 medium eggs
3 tbsp Marsala wine

FOR THE VINCISGRASSI (FILLING)
80g unsalted butter
1 shallot, peeled and finely sliced
200g pancetta, sliced
100g chestnut mushrooms, sliced
1 small truffle (jarred), drained and
    finely sliced
100ml chicken stock
950g chicken breast, finely sliced to
    thickness of little finger
300g chicken livers, sinew removed,
    roughly chopped
100g sweetbreads, sliced
4 tbsp Madeira
Salt and pepper to season
Small bunch of parsley, finely sliced
800ml béchamel sauce (page 146)
100g Parmesan, grated
50g pecorino, grated

CARMELA'S TIPS
This dish benefits from being made a day ahead as it will slice with ease if it has time to settle.

1 Make the pasta as you would normally (see page 13), but add the butter and Marsala along with the eggs. Combine, knead and wrap in cling film. Rest for a minimum of 30 minutes.
2 Once the dough is ready, roll it through your pasta machine into sheets approximately 10cm x 15cm.
3 Make the sauce. Place half the butter in a large shallow pan. Scatter in the shallots and fry gently over a medium heat for a couple of minutes.
4 Tumble in the pancetta and sliced mushrooms. Fry for 5 minutes until the mushrooms have softened and the pancetta has gained a little colour.
5 Add the thinly sliced truffle slices. Pour in the chicken stock and stir.
6 Add the chicken breast slices and fry for 4 minutes on each side.
7 Add the chicken livers and sweetbreads and cook for 5 minutes.
8 Pour in the Madeira. Cook for 3 minutes to reduce.
9 Season with salt and pepper and stir. Add the parsley.
10 Pour 400ml of the prepared béchamel sauce into the filling and stir.
11 Butter an ovenproof dish.
12 Lay pasta sheets over the base of the dish. Sprinkle over a little Parmesan and pecorino.
13 Ladle over some of the filling and cover the pasta.
14 Lay pasta sheets on top of the filling, sprinkle with Parmesan and pecorino and repeat, finishing with a layer of pasta.
15 Pinch small teaspoon-sized amounts of the remaining butter and place on the top layer of pasta.
16 Allow to cool, cover and chill overnight or for a few hours.
17 Top with the remaining 400ml béchamel sauce and bake at 200°C (gas 6) for 45 minutes to 1 hour, or until bubbling and golden. Once baked, cover and allow to rest for 10 minutes. Slice and serve.

LIGURIA

Liguria, situated in the northwest of Italy, is referred to as the Italian Riviera and without a doubt holds a very special place in my heart. If I could lose myself in Italy I think I would choose this region, a moon-shaped crescent, housing the beautifully quaint

▲ Liguria is fringed with busy fishing villages.

▶ Riomaggiore, a village in the province of La Spezia, Liguria – one of the towns of the Cinque Terre, a UNESCO World Heritage Site.

fishing villages of the Cinque Terre, described as a terrace overlooking the sea. Close your eyes for a moment, click your heels together and imagine brightly coloured houses perched over the warm Mediterranean sea, the hustle and bustle of busy fishing boats in the harbours.

Liguria not only oozes absolute beauty but is also known for some very different pasta shapes. Genoa the capital is where the very well-known basil pesto was born and here it is scrumptiously paired with delicately twisted *trofie* pasta. Wooden *corzetti* stamps also traditionally come from this region: circular stamps that usually have the family coat of arms or family crest carved into them, they are used to press circular discs of thin pasta dough that has been made with white wine. Oh, and yes, *sugeli* are the Ligurian version of *orecchiette* and a region that makes *orecchiette* certainly has my vote.

CORZETTI DISCS WITH A VEAL RAGU

CORZETTI AL RAGU DI VILETTO

As I mentioned in the introduction, *corzetti* pasta is a circular pressed flat pasta disc traditional to this region. Small wooden stamps are used in order to obtain the decorative design. In Liguria, the *corzetti* stamps are still made by hand. *Corzetti* pasta works incredibly well with a light sauce, a simple drizzle of seasonal pesto, a warm fresh tomato sauce or a slightly heavier veal sugo. Here I have opted for the slow-cooked veal sugo.

Preparation time 15 minutes
Cooking time 3 hours
Serves 4

360g *corzetti*, fresh or dried (page 23)
3 tbsp olive oil
1 carrot, peeled and diced
1 celery stalk, diced
1 medium onion, peeled and diced
700g veal mince
2 garlic cloves, peeled and roughly chopped
100ml red wine
1 tbsp tomato purée
2 x 680g bottles passata
Salt and pepper to season
Small bunch of basil leaves
80g Parmesan, grated

1 Pour the olive oil into a pan and place over a medium heat.

2 Tumble in the diced carrot, celery and onion. Stir with a wooden spoon until softened. Cook for approximately 10 minutes.

3 Add the veal mince and stir, breaking up any lumps. Cook for 5 minutes or so to colour all over.

4 Add the garlic and stir.

5 Pour in the red wine and allow to evaporate; this will only take a few minutes. I do love the aroma once the wine has been added.

6 Squeeze in the tomato purée and stir to coat the mince.

7 Pour in the two bottles of passata along with 300ml of water. I normally add water to the passata bottle and rinse them out into the sugo, so no passata is left behind. Season with salt and pepper. Add half the basil leaves.

8 Leave the sugo to bubble away over a low heat for 3 hours. Stir occasionally and check for seasoning.

9 Place a large pan of water on to boil. Once bubbling, salt well.

10 Cook the *corzetti* until al *dente*.

11 Drain the pasta and gently tip them back into the saucepan. Add a sprinkle of Parmesan and a ladle or two of sugo. Stir gently so that the discs do not tear.

12 Spoon the *corzetti* into bowls. Add a little more sugo to the bowls and an additional sprinkle of Parmesan and fresh basil leaves.

CARMELA'S TIPS
Corzetti stamps can easily be purchased online. Alternatively, use a small glass or cookie stamp to cut the dough into discs, just without the decoration.

HANDKERCHIEF PASTA WITH TEXTURED CREAMY PESTO

MANDILLI DI SETA

These elegant wafer-thin pasta handkerchiefs mimic folded silk honeymoon sheets and are draped in creamy pesto. The simplicity of the dish will without fail make it a regular on your weekly menu. My secret here is to add a little pasta water to the pesto base to give it a creamy texture. However, this dish does require freshly made pasta and I must add that delicate sheets only will do.

Preparation time 1 hour
Cooking time 15 minutes
Serves 4

FOR THE PASTA DOUGH
400g freshly prepared egg pasta dough
    (page 13)
Polenta, for dusting

FOR THE PESTO
3 large handfuls of basil
1 large clove garlic, peeled and
    roughly chopped
60g pine nuts, untoasted
70g Parmesan, grated (plus 30g for
    the table)
125ml extra virgin olive oil
Salt and pepper to season
Pasta water, to loosen

1 Place the basil leaves in your food processor along with the garlic, pine nuts and Parmesan. Whizz for 10 seconds.
2 Slowly add the extra virgin olive oil until you have reached the perfect dropping consistency. Taste and season with salt and pepper. Set aside until required.
3 Roll the pasta dough out in sections using a pasta machine to make thin sheets the thickness of a playing card.
4 Cut them into squares approximately 12cm x 12cm. Place the pasta squares onto a tea towel that has been lightly dusted with polenta.
5 Continue with the remaining dough. Allow the pasta handkerchiefs to dry for at least 15 minutes before cooking.
6 Place a large pan of water on to boil. Once boiling, salt well and cook the pasta for around 3 minutes until *al dente*.
7 Drain the pasta, reserving a ladle of water.
8 Place the pasta into a large pre-warmed serving dish. Add a couple of tablespoons of reserved pasta water to the pesto and stir well. Spoon the pesto onto the pasta and gently incorporate, adding a little more pasta water if required.
9 Serve in warm bowls with an additional grating of Parmesan on top.

LIGURIAN WILD HERB RAVIOLI WITH A CREAMY WALNUT PESTO

PANSOTTI AL PREBOGGION CON SALSA DI NOCI

Pansotti is another name for ravioli in the Liguria region of Italy and are triangular in shape. These pillows are filled with a mix of wild herbs called *preboggion* only found in Liguria. I have not had the pleasure of preparing these *pansotti* with the Ligurian wild herbs, so I use a combination of my own. I adore dandelion leaves and their overwhelming bitterness, combining them with spinach, Swiss chard, watercress, small oregano and marjoram leaves, chervil and basil to leave you with an aromatic taste of a fresh summer meadow.

Preparation time 1 hour 30 minutes
Cooking time 25 minutes
Serves 4

FOR THE PASTA DOUGH
400g fresh egg pasta (page 13)
70g Parmesan, grated
Polenta, for dusting

FOR THE PANSOTTI FILLING
300g (fresh weight) mixed herb leaves
600g ricotta
100g Parmesan grated
1 small garlic clove, peeled and
    finely crushed
1 egg
Pinch of nutmeg, freshly grated
Salt and pepper to season

FOR THE WALNUT PESTO
125ml milk
20g bread
130g walnuts, shelled and peeled
30g pine nuts, untoasted
1 garlic clove, peeled
60g Parmesan, grated
Small bunch of parsley, including stems
Salt and pepper to season
Olive oil
Basil and parsley, finely chopped

CARMELA'S TIPS
Prescinsêua is a traditional curd cheese made in Liguria and would be used to fill the *pansotti* instead of ricotta.

1 Place your mixed herbs and leaves (apart from the basil and chervil as they are too delicate) in a little water and blanch for 2 minutes. Drain and plunge in ice-cold water for 60 seconds. Drain again and then place on a clean tea towel and squeeze out all the excess water.

2 Add the basil and chervil to the blanched herbs and chop all the herbs finely.

3 Place the herbs, ricotta, Parmesan, garlic, egg, nutmeg, salt and pepper in a bowl. Stir to incorporate. Cover and chill until required (this filling can be made a day ahead if preferred).

4 To make the pesto, pour the milk into a bowl and add the bread. Leave to soften for 5 minutes.

5 Into a food processor, add the walnuts, pine nuts, garlic, Parmesan and parsley. Blitz for 10 seconds.

6 Add the softened bread and blitz for a further 10 seconds. The bread will add a delicious creaminess to the pesto.

7 Add a little olive oil until you reach a dropping consistency.

8 Taste and season with salt and pepper. If the sauce is a little thick don't worry as we will also add a little pasta water to loosen it when ready. Leave the pesto out at room temperature whilst you prepare the *pansotti*.

9 Make the *pansotti* (ravioli) following the instructions on page 18. Set aside on a lightly dusted tray with a sprinkle of polenta to prevent sticking.

10 Place a large pan of water on to boil. Once bubbling, salt well and add the *pansotti*. Allow the *pansotti* to cook until *al dente*. This will take about 4–5 minutes.

11 Drain, reserving a ladle of the pasta water.

12 Place the *pansotti* in a serving dish. Add the pesto along with some of the reserved pasta water and stir.

13 Spoon into bowls and scatter over a little extra Parmesan and a sprinkle of chopped basil and parsley.

TRENETTE WITH PESTO, GREEN BEANS AND POTATOES

TRENETTE AL PESTO

As a mother of four children there is nothing that excites me more than preparing an evening meal whilst using only one pot on the stove. Actually, the other thing that excites me a little about this recipe is carb on carb, pasta and potatoes. My father Rocco, however, doesn't feel the same. I think he still has a reccurring nightmare about being given this dish on far too many occasions whilst growing up. This recipe is completely different to the traditional 'Pasta e Patate' dish in my first cookbook, *Southern Italian Family Cooking*. *Trenette* is a flat long pasta also known as *fettuccine* and here it is paired beautifully with Genovese pesto, soft roasted new potatoes and green beans.

Preparation time 15 minutes
Cooking time 50 minutes
Serves 4

400g *trenette* pasta (fettuccine)
200g basil, leaves and stems
60g Parmesan, grated (plus 80g
    for the table)
60g pecorino, grated
60g pine nuts, untoasted
1 garlic clove, peeled
150ml extra virgin olive oil
Salt and pepper to season
250g green beans, trimmed at each end
250g new potatoes, skins on, halved
    and roasted
80g Parmesan, grated

1 Use a food processor to make the pesto. Add the basil leaves, stems, 60g Parmesan, pecorino, pine nuts, garlic and half the extra virgin olive oil. Blitz, then add the remaining oil until you have the perfect dropping consistency. Taste and season with salt and pepper.
2 Place a large pan of water on to boil for the pasta and green beans. Once the water is boiling, salt well.
3 Cook the pasta for 5 minutes then tumble in the green beans, stir and cook until both the pasta and the beans are *al dente*.
4 Drain, reserving a ladle of the starchy pasta water as this will later help to emulsify the sauce.
5 Place the pasta, green beans and warm roasted potatoes in a serving dish. Drizzle over all of the pesto and add a little pasta water. Stir well to encourage the sauce to turn slightly creamy.
6 Top with the remaining grated Parmesan and serve.

CARMELA'S TIPS

Trenette also works well with a sweet vongole sauce, carbonara (page 120) or a slightly more robust slow-cooked meat sauce (page 97).

TROFIE WITH CAVOLO NERO PESTO
TROFIE AL PESTO DI CAVOLO NERO

Trofie is a durum wheat pasta from Liguria. Traditionally, *trofie* is served with the famous *pesto alla Gevonese*, but here I wanted to share with you my cavolo nero pesto, which is a little stronger in flavour but truly exquisite. Cavolo nero, also known as black cabbage, is slightly prehistoric in texture with its bumpy almost scale-like leaves. A favourite in our home, it's incredibly versatile too, delicious stewed with shallots, garlic, chilli and tomatoes or used in the famous Tuscan soup *ribollita*. My favourite way of maximising this leaf is by making pesto: slightly more bitter than a traditional Gevonese pesto made solely with basil, but just as mouth-watering.

Preparation time 10 minutes
Cooking time 15 minutes
Serves 4

450g *trofie*
8 large leaves of cavolo nero
Large handful of basil
1 large clove garlic, peeled
60g pine nuts, untoasted
70g Parmesan, grated (plus extra for the table)
Extra virgin olive oil
Salt and pepper to season

1 Wash the cavolo nero and remove each side of the leaf from the stem. I gently tear the leaf away from the very firm centre stem but you can also use a knife or pair of kitchen scissors if preferred.
2 Place the cavolo nero into a pan of lightly salted water. Cook for 10 minutes until just tender.
3 Place a large pan of water on to boil for the *trofie*. Once boiling, salt well, add the *trofie* and cook until *al dente*.
4 Strain the cavolo nero then lay on a clean towel and squeeze the leaves to remove excess water (be firm).
5 Add the cavolo nero to your food processor along with the basil, garlic, pine nuts and Parmesan. Whizz for 10 seconds.
6 Slowly add the extra virgin olive oil until you have reached the perfect dropping consistency. Taste and season with salt and pepper.
7 Drain the pasta, reserving a ladle of water.
8 Place the pasta into a large pre-warmed serving dish. Add 4 tablespoons of pesto and stir. Add the reserved starchy pasta water and stir well. This will help to emulsify and make a deliciously creamy sauce. Add more pesto if required.
9 Serve in warm bowls with an additional grating of Parmesan on top.

CARMELA'S TIPS
You can use the traditional basil pesto here if you prefer, and kale would make a suitable replacement if cavolo nero is unavailable. If *trofie* are a little tricky to come by, then farfalle make a great alternative.

LOMBARDY
LOMBARDIA

▲ *Casoncelli* (see page 147), a delicate dish from Bergamo.

▶ An elevated view of Galleria Vittorio Emanuele II in Milan. Built in 1875, this gallery is one of the most popular shopping areas in the city.

Lombardy, happily situated in the north of Italy, is not only rich in culture but also has an abundance of surrounding influences. Its bordering regions include Piedmont, Veneto and Trentino. Grab your shiniest shoes and Sunday best, and set forth to Milan, not only the capital but also the fashion capital, stacked with designers shops and the most beautifully dressed Italians I have ever seen. My first visit to Lombardy was to its widest lake, Lake Garda some twelve years ago. I arranged a trip for my husband James' fortieth birthday, his first taste of Italy and certainly not his last.

Veal Milanese satisfies my ever-growing appetite every time I visit this region, along with my love of *casoncelli*, a type of filled pasta that are made in the shape of a half moon and then the dough slightly pushed inwards where the curve is (page 147).

BAKED RIGATONI WITH FOUR CHEESES
RIGATONI GRATINATI AI QUATTRO FORMAGGI

Close your eyes and prepare to immerse yourself mouth (and fork) first into the wonderland that is Italian cheese. This dish is not only comforting, warming and luscious, but also brings together some of my favourite cheeses from the region. Lombardy is the birthplace of Gorgonzola, delicious melted into this baked pasta dish, or try it melted with cream and Grana Padano and served with gnocchi. Try to imagine a life without cheese... I personally don't think it's possible!

Preparation time 30 minutes
Cooking time 1 hour
Serves 4

400g *rigatoni rigate* (ridged)
250g mozzarella, torn into pieces
200g fontina, slices
100g Gorgonzola, crumbled
Pinch of freshly grated nutmeg
Salt and pepper to season
3 tbsp fresh breadcrumbs
2 tbsp finely chopped parsley

FOR THE BÉCHAMEL SAUCE
100g unsalted butter, plus extra
  for greasing
50g '00' flour
700ml full fat milk
Salt and pepper to taste
100g Grana Padano, grated

1 Preheat the oven to 190°C (gas 5) and lightly butter a bakeware dish.
2 Place a large pan of water on to boil and when boiling salt well. Cook the pasta until very *al dente* (with a lot of bite). I normally cook this pasta for 5 minutes less than I normally would as it will be baked later.
3 Make the béchamel sauce. Warm the milk in a small saucepan until it reaches simmering point (this will take a couple of minutes).
4 In a small pan, melt the butter. Once melted, add the flour and stir vigorously with a wooden spoon, keeping the pan on the heat for a minute or so.
5 Slowly add the warm milk a little at a time, stirring slowly as you do and ensuring no lumps form.
6 Taste and season with a little salt and black pepper.
7 Place the béchamel back onto a low heat and slowly bring to the boil, whilst stirring, for 4 minutes until thickened.
8 Drain the pasta well.
9 Add the Grana Padano to the béchamel sauce and stir.
10 Spoon a layer of the béchamel sauce onto the base of the oven dish and then add a layer of pasta.
11 Sprinkle over half the mozzarella, fontina and Gorgonzola.
12 Add another layer of pasta then sprinkle a pinch of nutmeg and the remaining cheese on top.
13 Now add the final layer of pasta and pour over the remaining béchamel sauce.
14 Mix the breadcrumbs and finely chopped parsley together and sprinkle over the pasta.
15 Cover with foil and bake for 40 minutes, removing the foil for the last 20 minutes of cooking. Serve and enjoy.

CASONCELLI FROM BERGAMO

CASONCELLI ALLA BERGAMASCA

I would eat these *casoncelli* for breakfast, lunch and dinner if my waistline would allow. Delicate half-moon parcels from Bergamo (see page 144 for a photo), also known as *casonsei* in the local Bergamasco dialect, the ones in this recipe are filled with a mixed meat filling. Served with an uncomplicated *burro e salvia* (butter and sage) sauce, this dish highlights the absolute beauty that is freshly made pasta.

————————

Preparation time 1 hour
Cooking time 10 minutes
Serves 4

————————

FOR THE PASTA

400g freshly prepared egg pasta dough, rolled into thin lasagne sheets (page 13)

FOR THE FILLING

270g soft Italian sausage, cooked through
125g mortadella
90 stale breadcrumbs (soaked in
   3 tbsp milk)
1 garlic clove, peeled
1 large egg
1 tbsp fresh parsley
Salt and pepper to season

FOR THE SAUCE

80g unsalted butter
1 tbsp olive oil
300g *guanciale*, cut into small cubes
1 garlic clove, peeled and crushed
7 sage leaves
40g Grana Padano, grated
Small bunch of parsley, chopped,
   to finish

1 Put all the ingredients for the filling into a food processor. Blitz and set aside.

2 Place the lasagne sheets onto a lightly floured surface. Using a 6–7cm pastry cutter, press and cut out circles of dough.

3 Add a teaspoonful of the filling mixture onto each circle of dough. Fold and form into a half-moon (*mezzaluna*) and seal with a little water. Take the half-moons and gently press the curved centres in slightly and encourage the corners in a little.

4 Place the prepared *casoncelli* onto a tray dusted with a little polenta or semolina to eliminate sticking.

5 If time allows, allow the *casoncelli* to rest for a minimum of 30 minutes before cooking.

6 Place a large pan of water on to boil, salting well once boiling point has been reached.

7 Melt the butter and olive oil in a sauté pan. Add the *guanciale*, garlic and sage and cook over a medium heat. Lightly brown the *guanciale* but be careful to not burn the butter.

8 Cook the *casoncelli* for approximately 7 minutes. Drain and add to the sauté pan. Combine gently and serve with a generous dusting of Grana and a sprinkle of parsley.

PIZZOCCHERI WITH POTATOES AND CAVOLO NERO

PIZZOCCHERI ALLA VALTELLINESE

Pizzoccheri are short flat strips of pasta made with a combination of buckwheat flour and '00' flour and water. They are a speciality of the Valtellina valley in Lombardy, served with the local Valtellina Casera semi-hard cheese, potatoes and greens. I've chosen to use cavolo nero here because I simply adore this prehistoric-looking leaf. You could also use kale, spinach or escarole.

Preparation time 1 hour
Cooking time 20 minutes
Serves 4

FOR THE PASTA
400g buckwheat flour
100g '00' flour
250ml warm water

1.5 litres vegetable stock
250g potatoes, peeled and cubed
250g cavolo nero
85g unsalted butter
4 sage leaves
1 whole garlic clove, peeled
250g Valtellina Casera DOP cheese
125g Grana Padano
Black pepper to season

1 To make the the *pizzoccheri*, tumble the buckwheat flour and '00' flour onto a wooden board. Combine both flours and make a well in the centre.
2 Slowly add the water to the centre of the well. Gently combine the warm water and flour, form into a dough and knead until smooth and pliable. Cover and allow to rest for a minimum of 30 minutes at room temperature.
3 Lightly flour your surface and roll the dough out with a thin rolling pin to a thickness of 3mm. Cut strips of dough 10cm in length and a width of just over 1cm. Place the pasta onto a tea towel and set aside.
4 Take a large pan of vegetable stock and bring to the boil. Tumble in the potatoes and cavolo nero. Cook for 6 minutes (cavolo nero is a hardy leaf that benefits from overcooking).
5 Add the *pizzoccheri* to the potatoes and cavolo nero and cook for a further 10 minutes.
6 Meanwhile, melt the butter gently in a small frying pan with the garlic clove and sage leaves. Brown the butter.
7 Once the pizzoccheri are cooked, drain along with the vegetables. Spread half the *pizzoccheri*, potatoes and cavolo nero over the base of a warmed serving dish. Sprinkle generously with the Valtellina Casera cheese and then add another layer of the remaining *pizzoccheri* and vegetables over the top. Sprinkle over the remaining Valtellina Casera.
8 Remove the garlic clove from the browned butter and discard. Drizzle the butter over the *pizzoccheri*, add a twist of black pepper and some Grana cheese and serve.
9 The dish can be baked for 5 minutes to allow the cheese to melt. I however, prefer not to bake.

CARMELA'S TIPS
If you are unable to find Valtellina Casera, replace with the equally delicious fontina or taleggio. Once prepared, this dish can also be baked for 10 minutes so the cheese melts. I, however, prefer to tuck in immediately.

FILLED MEAT AGNOLINI FROM MILAN

AGNOLINI ALLA MILANESE

This *agnolini*, or ravioli, is a speciality from the fashion capital that is Milan. It's a fresh egg pasta filled with a mixture of slow-cooked meat and seasoning, served in a *brodo* (broth) or with browned butter and sage.
Try to plan ahead when making this dish as in my opinion the filling would benefit from being made a day or so in advance.

———

Preparation time 1 hour
Cooking time 2 hours 15 minutes
Serves 4

———

FOR THE PASTA DOUGH
400g prepared egg pasta dough
    (page 13)
Polenta or semolina, for dusting

FOR THE FILLING
1 tbsp olive oil
50g unsalted butter
1 sprig rosemary
200g beef mince
150g veal or pork mince
80g pancetta, chopped finely
200ml water or chicken stock
1 medium egg
70g Grana Padano, grated
½ tsp cinnamon
Salt and pepper to season

FOR THE SAUCE
50g unsalted butter
4 sage leaves, sliced
1 garlic clove, peeled and halved
30g Grana Padano, grated

1 Into a large pan over a medium heat, add the olive oil and butter.
2 Stir, then add the rosemary sprig along with the beef, veal mince and pancetta. Brown all over for 5 minutes.
3 Pour the water or stock into the pan, cover and allow to cook on a low heat for 2 hours. Keep an eye on the meat and if it looks as though it's drying out, add a little more water.
4 Once cooked, drain the meat, reserving the liquid.
5 Place the cooked mincemeat onto a board and chop it finely if required. If not, just transfer the meat directly to a bowl. Add the egg, 70g Grana, cinnamon and a twist of salt and pepper. Stir and taste for additional seasoning. Add a tablespoon of reserved liquid if needed to combine the ingredients. Cover and refrigerate until required.
6 Roll the pasta dough into thin lasagne sheets (see page 13).
7 Drop small teaspoonfuls of the filling onto one side of the pasta sheet lengthways, remembering you have to fold the sheet over. Place the filling at 4cm intervals.
8 Using your fingertips, dampen the pasta around each heap of filling, then fold the dough over, forming into ravioli pillows and pushing out any air and bubbles.
9 Use a fluted pastry wheel to cut the ravioli into individual shapes.
10 Repeat until all of the filling and pasta dough has been used up.
11 Set the ravioli aside on a tray dusted with polenta or semolina to prevent the pasta from sticking. Allow them to rest for 30 minutes. I intermittently turn them over as they still have a tendency to stick.
12 Place a large pan of water on to boil for the pasta. Once boiling, salt well, add the pasta and cook for 3–4 minutes.
13 Add the butter, sage and garlic to a small frying pan over a medium heat. Add 3 tablespoons of the reserved pasta water to help emulsify the sauce. After 4 minutes remove the sauce from the heat and discard the garlic.
14 Drain the pasta and stir gently into the butter and sage sauce.
15 Serve in bowls with a dusting of Grana Padano.

PUMPKIN AND AMARETTI TORTELLI

TORTELLI DI ZUCCA

This recipe is for all of my friends who believe I have something of a love affair with amaretti, whether it be in biscuit or liquid (amaretto) form. This combination is beyond heavenly and is a favourite dish of my good friend Julie, who fell in love with this sweet and savoury pasta dish on a recent trip to Italy. I believe her words were, 'I never want this meal to end'. Like everything in life it must come to an end, but meanwhile here is a beautiful recipe to replicate at home.

Preparation time 1 hour 30 minutes
Cooking time 40 minutes
Serves 4

400g prepared egg pasta dough

FOR THE FILLING

1kg pumpkin, deseeded and cut
    into wedges
90g hard amaretti biscuits, crushed
150g Grana Padano, grated
100g *mostarda di frutta* (spicy jarred
    fruit), finely chopped into tiny pieces
Freshly grated nutmeg
Zest of 1 small lemon
Salt and pepper to season

FOR THE SAUCE

1 tbsp olive oil
90g unsalted butter
8 sage leaves
70g Grana Padano, grated
30g hard amaretti, crushed (optional)

1 Start by making the filling. Roast the prepared pumpkin in an oven preheated to 190°C (gas 5) for 30 minutes until tender.

2 Remove the pumpkin from the oven, push through a sieve and allow the smooth pulp to cool for an hour.

3 Mix the pulp along with the 90g crushed amaretti biscuits, the Grana Padano, *mostarda di frutta*, nutmeg and lemon. Taste and season with salt and pepper.

4 Cover the mixture and set aside.

5 Roll the dough out with either a rolling pin or using your pasta machine, which should be sitting proudly on your kitchen surface. I normally roll the dough out into manageable portions using my pasta machine and then form the dough into lasagne sheets by hand.

6 Place the lasagne sheets onto a lightly floured surface. Cut them into squares measuring approximately 4cm x 4cm.

7 Place a teaspoonful of the mixture onto each square. Using a little water on your fingertips, dampen the corners of the dough and fold each square into a triangle, gently squeezing out any air.

8 Hold the triangle with the point facing upwards and join each of the two lower corners together to form a perfect, or for me slightly wobbly, *tortello*. Repeat with the remaining dough and filling.

9 Bring a large pan of water to a boil. Once boiling, salt well, add the pasta and cook for 4 minutes until *al dente*.

10 Pour the oil into a frying pan and add the butter along with the sage leaves. Brown for 3 minutes.

11 Drain the pasta and spoon into warmed bowls. Add a delicate drizzle of the browned butter.

12 Add a final sprinkle of Grana Padano. I love to also add an additional amaretti crumble to finish the dish.

MOLISE

Molise is nestled on the borders of Abruzzo and Puglia and is the second smallest region in Italy. Is Molise somewhat forgotten, a lesser-known region, not as touristy and visited as its slightly more recognised neighbours? Or is it simply a pass-through region? Many years ago, it certainly was. You would drive through Molise to reach either Puglia or Abruzzo.

My mamma Solidea's side of the family are from this region, from the region's capital Campobasso and from the small quaint hillside village of Oratino. The region itself isn't a region rich in work, but it is certainly rich in tradition and passionate about family and food. Simple family mealtime dishes of filled pasta shells, lasagne filled with a rich sugo and boiled eggs, to simple pasta with butter. Molise evokes *cucina povera* cooking in so many ways. The influences of the style of cooking have certainly shaped the way my mum cooks and clearly these traits have been passed on to me.

▲ Ancient fishing machine known as a *trabucco* stretches out into the Adriatic near Termoli, Molise.

▶ The old town of Termoli, Molise.

CAVATELLI PASTA WITH MUSHROOMS AND SAUSAGE

CAVATELLI CON FUNGHI E SALCICHIA

This recipe really reminds me of my Nonna Carmela and mum Solidea, not so much for the sauce but for the pasta shape and the way it is made. *Cavatelli* are made by indenting one, two or three fingertips into small pieces of dough, leaving small dents perfect for catching the sauce. *Cavatelli* are also known in the region as *cuzze* or *cuzzettielle*.

Preparation time 1 hour
Cooking time 25 minutes
Serves 4

400g *cavatelli*
500g mushrooms, mixed (your choice)
4 tbsp olive oil
250g soft Italian sausages,
    roughly chopped
2 garlic cloves, peeled and finely sliced
1 x 680g bottle passata
Pinch of dried oregano
Small bunch of basil, roughly torn
Small bunch of parsley, chopped
Pinch of dried chilli (optional)
Salt and pepper to season
70g Parmesan, grated

1 Brush the mushrooms with a clean cloth. Do not wash them as they mimic little sponges. Slice the mushrooms.
2 Pour the oil into a large shallow pan and bring to a medium heat. Add the sausage and cook for 7 minutes until browned all over.
3 Add the mushrooms and garlic to the pan. Stir and cook for an additional 5 minutes.
4 Pour in the passata along with 150ml of water. I normally swirl out the passata jar with the water.
5 Add the oregano, half the fresh herbs and a sprinkle of chilli. Season well with salt and black pepper. Cook for 20 minutes.
6 Place a large pan of water on to boil. Once boiling, salt well, add the *cavatelli* and cook until *al dente*.
7 Drain the pasta, reserving a ladle of the pasta water.
8 Add the pasta to the sauce along with the reserved water, and stir.
9 Scatter over the remaining fresh herbs. Stir and serve with a sprinkle of Parmesan.

CARMELA'S TIPS
I love *ricotta salata* (salted ricotta) grated generously over this dish.

PASTA SHELLS FILLED WITH RICOTTA AND MOZZARELLA

CONCHIGLIONI RIPIENE CON RICOTTA E MOZZARELLA

If lasagne isn't on the menu when we visit my parents, then I can normally be assured of finding these beautifully rounded shells, bursting to the brim, instead. This recipe for *conchiglioni* is one of my mother Solidea's trump cards and one of my family's favourite baked pasta dishes and I urge you to indulge yourself. The *conchiglioni* – large shells – are filled and baked in the oven. The pork mince can be easily substituted with fresh spinach or blanched cavolo nero to make a delicious vegetarian version.

Preparation time 25 minutes
Cooking time 1 hour
Serves 6

500g large *conchiglioni* shells
500g minced pork
500g mozzarella, grated or chopped
700g ricotta
Pinch of nutmeg, freshly grated
100g Parmesan, grated
3 garlic cloves, peeled and crushed
Salt and pepper to season
3 large eggs
4 tbsp parsley, chopped
800ml simple tomato sauce (page 226)
  or bottled

1 Preheat the oven to 190°C (gas 5).
2 Brown off the minced pork in a frying pan and, when coloured, drain off any excess fat and allow to cool slightly.
3 Place a large pan of water on to boil for the pasta shells and once the water is bubbling add a tablespoon of salt. Cook the *conchiglioni* shells for 9–10 minutes (3 minutes less than the packet instructions specify).
4 Meanwhile, for the filling, combine the mozzarella, ricotta, nutmeg, Parmesan (reserving a little to sprinkle on top), garlic, salt and pepper in a large bowl and mix well. Add three large eggs and stir. Now add the pork that has been drained of fat and cooled slightly. Scatter in the chopped parsley and stir again.
5 Add 2 ladles of the tomato sauce to the filling so that it adds colour and a little texture to the mixture. Stir to combine.
6 In a 30cm x 30cm ovenproof dish, spoon two small ladles of sauce to cover the base.
7 Drain the *conchiglioni* shells, then begin to fill them with the pork filling and place in the ovenproof dish. Once the whole dish is bursting with shells, pour over a couple of ladles of sauce. Sprinkle over the remaining Parmesan.
8 Cover the pasta with foil and bake for 45 minutes, then remove the foil and cook for a further 15 minutes until bubbling, golden and ready to enjoy.
9 Serve on warmed plates with a basket of fresh bread and a seasonal salad.

SPAGHETTI WITH SQUID
SPAGHETTI CON CALAMARI

Can you smell the aroma? Just by reading the title I feel a childlike smile spread across my face. Traditionally served on Christmas Eve but equally good on any day of the year, this sauce showcases Italian cooking and simplicity at its best. Calamari would either normally need to be cooked very quickly or simmered slowly to avoid it becoming too tough and chewy. For me, this dish evokes memories of my father Rocco and the night before Christmas, when the smell would permeate through the house and the excitement would begin. I do love food memories.

Preparation time 10 minutes
Cooking time 1 hour 25 minutes
Serves 4

400g dried spaghetti
250g cleaned calamari, sliced, with
    tentacles
2 tbsp olive oil
2 cloves garlic, peeled and crushed
1 x 680g bottle passata
50ml water
Handful of fresh basil, torn
Salt and pepper to season
1 tsp dried chilli flakes (optional)

1 Wash the prepared calamari and slice into 2.5cm pieces.

2 Add the olive oil to a saucepan and heat to a moderate temperature.

3 Add the calamari slices and tentacles. Stir whilst cooking for 2 minutes.

4 Add the garlic to the calamari along with a pinch of salt.

5 Pour in the passata along with the water and stir.

6 Add a generous amount of basil, stir and leave to simmer gently for 1 hour 25 minutes.

7 Fifteen minutes before the sauce is ready, cook the spaghetti in salted water according to the packet instructions, minus 2 minutes to ensure the spaghetti remains *al dente*.

8 Drain the pasta and add a little sauce to colour the golden strands.

9 Spoon the spaghetti into bowls then gently arrange the calamari over and through the pasta.

PASTA SHELLS WITH BUTTER AND PANCETTA

CONCHIGLIETTE CON BURRO E PANCETTA

Small pasta shells with browned butter and pancetta – this dish is speedy, inexpensive, easy-to-make and oh so tasty. Southern Italy is all about eating well for less, using the store cupboard to produce a family meal for a minimal cost. You can change the shape of pasta, but always choose a shape that can hold and cup the butter and pancetta.

Preparation time 5 minutes
Cooking time 10 minutes
Serves 4

400g *conchigliette* (tiny pasta shells)
125g unsalted butter, diced
250g pancetta, sliced or diced
Salt and pepper to season
1 tbsp parsley, chopped

1 Bring a pan of water to a boil for the pasta. Once boiling, salt well.
2 Add the pasta and cook according to the packet instructions, minus 2 minutes to ensure the pasta remains *al dente*.
3 In a frying pan, melt the diced butter and gently fry the pancetta until it is lightly golden, for around 5–7 minutes, being careful to not burn the butter.
4 Drain the pasta and tumble into the frying pan. Season with salt and pepper and sprinkle over the chopped parsley, then stir to combine the pasta with the sauce.
5 Serve in warm bowls.

SOLIDEA'S EGG-LAYERED LASAGNE

LASAGNA

It would be impossible for me to write a book on pasta and not include my mum Solidea's recipe for egg-layered lasagne. Lasagne is a regional dish from La Campagnia, but as you may be aware each region has their own take on this very popular family favourite. This recipe is from Campobasso, capital of Molise. Laced with chopped boiled eggs, slow-cooked mincemeat sugo and lots of freshly torn mozzarella and grated Parmesan, this lasagne has no béchamel sauce but just a final scatter of mozzarella and light snowfall of Parmesan. My desert island dish.

Preparation time 40 minutes
Cooking time 4 hours 30 minutes
Serves 10–12

18 freshly made lasagne sheets
   (or 2 x boxes dried)

FOR THE SAUCE (SUGO)
700g pork mince
700g beef mince
3 garlic cloves, peeled and crushed
100g tomato purée
4 x 680g bottles tomato passata
300ml water
Handful of basil, torn

FOR THE LASAGNE
6 large eggs, boiled
2 large eggs, beaten
500g mozzarella, grated
80g Parmesan, grated

1 Start by making the sugo. Fry the beef and pork mince in a large saucepan for approximately 5–7 minutes until browned. Remove any excess cooking fat and return to the heat.
2 Add the garlic and tomato purée to the pan, and stir.
3 Pour in the passata along with the water and stir again, then season with salt and pepper. Scatter over the basil and simmer for 2 hours 30 minutes.
4 When the sugo is ready, preheat the oven to 170°C (gas 4) and start to assemble the lasagne. You will need a large ovenproof dish, 30cm x 40cm.
5 Chop the boiled eggs.
6 Place 3 small ladlefuls of the passata mince sauce into the ovenproof dish, covering the base, and then add a layer of lasagne pasta sheets on top.
7 Sprinkle over some mozzarella, chopped egg and, using a fork, drizzle over some of the beaten egg to bind the filling.
8 Repeat this process layer by layer. Finish the lasagne with a layer of mince sauce and a grating of mozzarella. Sprinkle over the Parmesan.
9 Cover with foil and bake for 1 hour 15 minutes. Remove the foil and cook for a further 15 minutes to allow the lasagne to brown.
10 Switch off the oven and let the lasagne stand for 15 minutes before slicing. I find that the best way to do this is to leave the lasagne in the oven but with the door slightly ajar.
11 Slice and serve.

CARMELA'S TIPS
You can cut down the cooking time considerably if you make the sugo a day or so in advance. You can also add veal mince to the sugo base for added richness; just reduce the amount of pork and beef. Lasagne freezes well too, so cook in half batches in aluminium trays and freeze for up to three months.

PIEDMONT

PIEMONTE

Piedmont borders France and Switzerland. The meaning of the name is 'at the foot of a mountain' – and yes, that's exactly where this region is positioned, at the base of the Alps. Piedmont has beautiful attractions, stunning views and spectacular valleys. The region is rich in food, famous for its full-bodied Barolo wine, amazing cheeses, truffles and regional classic dishes.

The traditional pasta of the region is a handmade long flat spaghetti known as *tajerin*, as well as *agnolotti*, a type of ravioli. The capital of Piedmont is Turin, which is known as the Italian car-manufacturing city. Piedmont's other claim to fame is that it is where Antonio Carluccio grew up. He is known as the godfather (*Il Padrino*) of Italian food and some of my inspiration comes from him.

▲ *Agnolotti* pasta is a favourite dish in Piedmont, with a variety of fillings and sauces.

▶ The island of San Guilio, named for the patron saint of Piedmont, sits in Lake Orta.

PAPPARDELLE WITH A BARBARESCO SAUCE

PAPPARDELLE AL BARBARESCO

This dish sums up the region of Piedmont for me. The only ingredient missing here would be the pungent truffles from beautiful Alba. However, here we have ruby red wine paired with autumnal mushrooms and either pappardelle or tagliatelle. Altogether, this makes for a warming yet indulgently robust bowl of Piemontese satisfaction.

Preparation time 20 minutes
Cooking time 40 minutes
Serves 4

350g fresh pappardelle or dried
50g unsalted butter
1 tbsp olive oil
2 banana shallots, peeled and finely
    chopped
1 garlic clove, peeled and crushed
Small bunch of parsley, finely chopped
    (including stems)
225g mixed mushrooms of your choice
50g tomato purée
250ml Barbaresco red wine
Salt and pepper to season
A few sprigs of fresh thyme (reserve a
    few leaves to finish)
60g freshly toasted breadcrumbs
50g Parmesan, grated

1 Spoon the butter into a large sauté pan along with the olive oil over a medium heat.
2 Add the shallots and stir until they have softened and start to appear translucent.
3 Scrape in the garlic and stir.
4 Scatter in the parsley and stir again.
5 Ensure the mushrooms are clean and free from grit. Never run them under water as they act like little sponges. Simply wipe them with a clean cloth and give them a gentle blow. Slice the mushrooms and add them to the pan. Cook for 4 minutes until they begin to relax a little.
6 Stir and then add the tomato purée followed by the wine.
7 Season with salt and pepper and add a sprig of thyme. Cook for 25 minutes. Stir and adjust seasoning if required. Feel free to add a pinch of chilli if you like it hot.
8 Place a large pan of water on to boil. Once boiling, salt well, add the pasta and cook until *al dente*.
9 Place the warm toasted breadcrumbs, thyme and Parmesan into a small bowl and stir.
10 Drain the pasta, reserving a small ladle of starchy pasta water.
11 Add the pappardelle along with the reserved pasta water to the mushroom sauce and stir.
12 Spoon into warm bowls and sprinkle over the seasoned breadcrumb mix.

CARMELA'S TIPS
Barolo wine works well here too. However, please feel free to use whatever you prefer.

RAVIOLI PILLOWS FILLED WITH VEAL

AGNOLOTTI DEL PLIN

Agnolotti is the Piedmont name for ravioli, just to save any confusion.
I love the name of this dish – *plin* simply means 'pinching' to seal the
dough between your forefinger and thumb. All over the region the fillings
will vary as will the sauce topping. I have used a combination of my
favourite meats here. The filling really does benefit from being made
the day before to allow the flavours to develop.

Preparation time 1 hour 20 minutes
Cooking time 2 hours 10 minutes
Serves 4

FOR THE PASTA
400g freshly prepared egg pasta dough
    (page 13)
Polenta, for dusting

FOR THE FILLING
30g unsalted butter
2 tbsp olive oil
1 stick celery, cut into small dice
1 carrot, peeled and cut into small dice
1 medium white onion, peeled and
    cut into small dice
2 garlic cloves, peeled and finely sliced
300g loin of veal, chopped into
    small pieces
200g boned shoulder pork, chopped
    into small pieces
200g sausage meat, skinned and
    roughly chopped
2 tbsp tomato purée
125ml red wine
1 litre vegetable stock
Salt and pepper to season
250g spinach, blanched and
    finely chopped
70g Parmesan (plus extra for the table)
Freshly grated nutmeg
2 egg yolks

FOR THE SAUCE
3 tbsp butter
50ml cooking juices
4 sage leaves

1 To make the filling, melt the butter and olive oil in a large shallow pan.
2 Tumble the celery, carrot, onion and garlic into the pan and cook over a
low heat for 10 minutes.
3 Add the veal, pork and sausage and stir. Cook for around 10 minutes to
sear the meat all over,
4 Add the tomato purée, red wine and vegetable stock. Season with salt
and pepper. Cover and allow to cook over a medium heat for 2 hours.
Check every 20 minutes for seasoning.
5 Once the meat is cooked, drain any juices and reserve.
6 Pour all of the contents of the pan into a food processor and blitz gently.
7 Add the blanched and tightly squeezed spinach, Parmesan, nutmeg and
egg yolks. Blitz for 30 seconds.
8 Stir, taste and check for seasoning.
9 Spoon into a bowl, cover and chill.
10 Roll the pasta dough out into long lasagne sheets with a pasta machine.
Cut the dough into 15cm widths and spoon a little of the chilled filling
mixture in mounds along the centre of the dough at 3cm intervals.
11 Fold one side of dough over the filling, and encourage the dough to
sit around the filling with no trapped or air bubbles. Fold over the other
section of dough.
12 Pinch the dough in between each *agnolotti* mound; this is what makes
them special and from Piedmont.
13 Cut each *agnolotti* along the sealed edge. Place on a tray of lightly
dusted polenta and continue with the remaining dough.
14 Place a large pan of water on to boil. Once boiling, salt well and cook
the *agnolotti* until cooked through and *al dente* (4 minutes).
15 For the sauce, add the butter to a sauté pan along with the sage leaves
and 50ml of the reserved cooking juices. Cook for 5 minutes.
16 Drain the *agnolotti* and, using a slotted spoon, place them in the sauce.
17 Spoon into warm bowls and serve with extra Parmesan.

TAJERIN WITH BUTTER AND WHITE TRUFFLE

TAJERIN AL BURRO E TARTUFO BIANCO

Tajerin, known as *taglierini* elsewhere in Italy, are flat, very thin pasta strands that love a light sauce but also are happy paired with a tomato sauce. This dish is really all about the famous white truffle. On my bucket list, I'd very much love to go truffle hunting with Antonio Carluccio. My basket is always ready, Antonio! Until then... These white truffles are difficult to come by, so a little cheating will be necessary. Use either truffle butter or preserved truffles, finely sliced to give you the truffle hit needed to make you feel you are in Piedmont.

Preparation time 1 hour
Cooking time 10 minutes
Serves 4

FOR THE PASTA DOUGH
340g '00' flour
6 large egg yolks
Polenta, for dusting

FOR THE SAUCE
80g unsalted butter
Small bunch of parsley, finely chopped
80g Parmesan
Salt and pepper to season
Freshly sliced white truffle or white truffle oil, to drizzle

1 To make the *tajerin* pasta by hand, make a volcano of flour on a wooden board and add the egg yolks to the centre. Using a fork or your fingertips, combine the eggs with the flour. If the dough is a little dry add a tablespoon or two of water. Knead until smooth and elastic. Cover and set aside for a minimum of 30 minutes. (Freeze the egg white to make a meringue or pavlova at a later date.)

2 Roll out the dough (in sections) as described on page 13 and using your pasta machine with the small cutting blades, cut the pasta into delicate strands. I call them angel hairs as the pasta is so thin. Place the cut *tajerin* onto a tray that has been lightly dusted with polenta. Continue in the same way with the remaining pasta dough.

3 Bring a large pan of water to the boil. Once boiling, salt well and cook the *tajerin* for a couple of minutes.

4 Melt the butter in a small frying pan and add the parsley.

5 Drain the pasta and transfer it to a warmed bowl.

6 Pour over the melted butter.

7 Add the Parmesan and stir. Season with a little salt and pepper.

8 Add a few shavings of fresh truffle or a few drops of truffle oil and serve.

CARMELA'S TIPS
You can also use 400g dried *taglierini* pasta instead of making your own, if preferred.

TAJARIN WITH CHICKEN LIVERS

TAJARIN CON FEGATINI

'Liver and onions, Italian style' – this is exactly how my photographer Helen described this dish when she photographed it and she is totally correct. Chicken liver sauce is not only inexpensive but also quick to prepare and incredibly delicious – and I must say a favourite of my offal-loving husband.

———

Preparation time 10 minutes
Cooking time 20 minutes
Serves 4

———

400g *tajarin* (*taglierini*) pasta, dried or
    fresh (page 170)
60g unsalted butter
2 tbsp olive oil
2 small banana shallots, peeled and
    finely sliced
300g chicken livers, sinews removed and
    cut into thin slices
1 tbsp tomato purée
200ml chicken stock
2 tbsp Marsala
Salt and pepper to season
6 sage leaves, sliced
80g Parmesan, grated (optional)

1 Melt the butter and olive oil in a shallow pan.
2 Scatter in the shallots and stir with a wooden spoon until softened and translucent in colour.
3 Add the sliced chicken livers and stir. Sear and colour lightly.
4 Squeeze in the tomato purée, stir and pour in the chicken stock. Cook for 10 minutes.
5 Place a large pan of water on to boil for the pasta. Once boiling, salt well.
6 Pour the Marsala into the chicken livers, season with salt and pepper and scatter in the sage leaves. Cook for a further 10 minutes.
7 Cook the pasta until *al dente* (it will only take a couple of minutes).
8 Drain the pasta and add the strands to the liver sauce. Stir and serve immediately with a little Parmesan if desired.

TAJARIN WITH FONTINA FONDUE AND TRUFFLE OIL

TAJERIN CON FONDUTA E OLIO DI TARTUFO

Cheese fondue anyone? *Fonduta* is a favourite of the Piedmont region. As a cheese lover, this sauce alone is a staple around my family table. A bowl of warmed fontina, eggs and milk, it's gooey, oozy and absolutely moreish. I love to dip toasted bread or chicory leaves into the cheese, great for sharing at a dinner party. In this dish the pasta is coated with the glossy fontina sauce and there's a pungent aroma of truffle oil. Just be patient while preparing as you don't want to scramble the mixture.

Preparation time 10 minutes
Cooking time 1 hour 20 minutes
Serves 4

400g *tajarin* (*taglierini*) pasta, dried or
    fresh (page 170)
450g fontina cheese, cut into small cubes
2 pints milk
30g unsalted butter
5 large egg yolks
Salt and pepper to season
Truffle oil, to drizzle

1 Place the fontina cheese in a bowl.

2 Pour the milk over the fontina and allow it to stand for 1 hour.

3 Melt the butter in a heavy-based pan over a low heat.

4 Slowly add the fontina and milk.

5 Stir and whisk constantly until the fontina starts to melt and you can visibly see the fontina strands.

6 Be patient. Slowly increase the heat and continue whisking. Add one egg yolk at a time and incorporate. At this stage the mixture could easily scramble and catch on the bottom of the pan.

7 Place a large pan of water on to boil for the pasta. Once boiling, salt well and cook the pasta, which will only take a couple of minutes.

8 Once all of the eggs have been added to the *fonduta*, check for seasoning and add salt and pepper as required.

9 Drain the pasta and return it to the pan.

10 Add the *fonduta* sauce to the pasta, stir and serve with a light drizzle of truffle oil or a little grated white truffle.

PUGLIA
APULIA

One of the flattest regions in Italy and with an astonishing coastline of around 500 miles, Puglia, in the heel of Italy, is famed for its beautiful cone-shaped dry-stone houses (*trulli*). Just thinking about Puglia instantly makes me hungry for copious amounts of fresh seafood, fish, vegetables warmed by the midday sun and served with traditional handmade pasta.

The region is very close to my heart as it is where my father Rocco's family are from: a small village called Castellucio Vallmaggiore very close to the boarder of Campagnia in the province of Foggia. Castellucio Vallmaggiore is a village that tends to feed on the dry rugged land, as does much of the south of Italy, on fruit, vegetables and hand-reared pigs, sheep and goats. Being inland, fish and seafood would probably only feature on our family table once or twice a week, on market days.

▲ Strascinati pasta is very simple to make. (See page 182 for the recipe.)

▶ *Trulli* houses in Alberobello, Puglia, have delightfully quirky conical roofs.

As a large region, the style of cooking throughout varies dramatically. Puglia has so much to offer, from the most fabulous extra virgin olive oil to an array of exquisite cheeses, including my favourite, *burrata*, and not forgetting the famous pasta of the region, *orecchiette*. As I've mentioned before, Puglia is known, as is the south of Italy, for its unique style of cooking, *cucina povera*.

FILLED AND ROLLED BEEF AND PORK WITH CICATELLI

SUGO DI BRACIOLE CON CICATELLI FATTO A MANO

I simply adore this dish because you benefit fully from a two-course meal: pasta with *braciole* sugo, followed by more *braciole* – escalopes of beef and pork that are battened out, seasoned with fresh herbs and garlic, then rolled, pan fried and slowly cooked – and salad. *Cicatelli* pasta is used here. Made by hand with semolina flour, hot water and working hands, *cicatelli* are also known as *cavatelli*.

Preparation time 1 hour
Cooking time 2 hours 30 minutes
Serves 4

400g prepared cicatelli pasta (page 29)

FOR THE BRACIOLE
4 beef escalopes
4 pork escalopes
3 garlic cloves, peeled and crushed
20 basil leaves, finely sliced
Pinch of dried oregano
1 small chilli, deseeded, finely sliced
Salt and pepper to season
6 tbsp olive oil

FOR THE SAUCE
1 shallot, peeled and finely sliced
1 garlic clove, peeled and crushed
1 tbsp tomato purée
125ml red wine
2 x 680g bottles passata
100ml water
1 small Parmesan rind
Small bunch of basil, roughly torn
100g Parmesan, grated

1 To make the *braciole*, use a meat tenderiser to gently pound the meat a little being careful to not tear it.
2 Into a small bowl, add the crushed garlic, basil leaves, oregano, chilli, salt, pepper and 2 tablespoons of olive oil. Stir and spread a little over each of the escalopes until all of the paste is used.
3 Roll each of the escalopes into small sausages and secure each one with two cocktail sticks.
4 Take a large pan and add the remaining olive oil. Sear the escalopes in batches until lightly browned all over.
5 Remove the *braciole* from the pan and add the shallot and garlic. Fry off for 2 minutes.
6 Place the *braciole* back into the pan and squeeze in the tomato purée and stir.
7 Pour in the red wine, stir and allow to reduce for 2 minutes.
8 Add the passata, water and Parmesan rind.
9 Season with salt, pepper and tumble in half the basil. Cook over a low heat for 2 hours 30 minutes. Stir and check for additional seasoning intermittently.
10 Cook the *cicatelli* in a large pan of salted water.
11 Add the remaining basil to the sauce.
12 Drain and tumble the *cicatelli* back into the pan. Add 50g of Parmesan and 2 ladles of sugo (sauce).
13 Stir and spoon into warmed bowls. Top with a little extra sugo and more grated Parmesan.
14 Keep the *braciole* warm and on standby for your second course.

CARMELA'S TIPS
Serve the *braciole* after the pasta with a freshly tossed salad, green beans dressed with garlic and extra virgin olive oil and fresh Pugliese bread.

FRIED PASTA WITH CHICK PEAS

CICERI E TRIA

Another worthy dish from the Salento region of Puglia, I love this dish as it really is so different in texture to many other dishes from the south of Italy. *Ciceri* means chickpea and *tria* is an old Arabic word for pasta – so much history in a humble bowl of pasta. Here around one third of the pasta is fried and placed on top of the final dish. You can use dried chickpeas and soak them overnight. However, I tend to stockpile tins for ease.

Preparation time 1 hour
Cooking time 25 minutes
Serves 4

FOR THE PASTA DOUGH
150g '00' flour
250g semolina flour
(*semola di grano duro*)
200ml hot water

FOR THE SAUCE
4 tbsp olive oil
1 medium carrot, peeled and finely
    chopped
1 celery stick plus leaves, finely chopped
1 medium white onion, peeled and
    finely chopped
1 garlic clove, peeled and finely sliced
1 bay leaf
2 large tomatoes, roughly chopped
1 x 400g tin chickpeas
Pinch of chilli flakes
Salt and pepper to season
Small bunch of parsley, roughly chopped
Small bunch of basil, roughly chopped
200ml olive oil for frying
80g pecorino, grated
Extra virgin olive oil, to drizzle

CARMELA'S TIPS
Barley flour is normally used here, along with semolina flour. I have used '00' flour instead, as I prefer the taste. The pasta could be made a day in advance to speed up the method.

1 Pour the '00' flour and semolina flour onto a wooden board, mix together, then make a well in the centre.
2 Add the water gradually and begin to incorporate the flour using a fork, or your fingertips if preferred, until you have a pasta dough consistency.
3 Knead for 5 minutes until smooth and elastic. Cover with cling film and allow the dough to rest for a minimum of 30 minutes.
4 Roll the dough out with a long thin rolling pin to the thickness of a 10p piece. Cut the dough into strips of around 8cm x 2cm. Place the strips onto trays and dry for at least 1–2 hours.
5 Meanwhile, pour the olive oil into a shallow pan, place on a medium heat and add the carrot, celery, onion and garlic. Fry off gently for 10 minutes until tender.
6 Add the bay leaf and tomatoes. Stir and season with a little chilli, salt and pepper; stir.
7 Tumble in the drained chickpeas and half the fresh herbs. Stir and allow to simmer on a low heat for 15 minutes.
8 Place a large pan of water on to boil. When boiling, salt well and cook two thirds of the pasta until *al dente*.
9 Into a medium frying pan, pour the frying oil (about 1cm deep) and fry the reserved pasta in small batches until coloured lightly on both sides (30 seconds or so on each side). Drain on kitchen towel and repeat.
10 Drain and add the cooked pasta to the chickpeas along with the remaining fresh herbs and stir.
11 Spoon into bowls with a scattering of the fried pasta, a glug of extra virgin olive oil and a sprinkle of pecorino.

MINCHIAREDDHI WITH SEAFOOD

MINCHIAREDDHI ALLA PESCADOR

Salento is located right at the heel of Puglia and this is a dish that
the town is very proud of, amongst others of course. Minchiareddhi
(*maccaruni*) is a homemade pasta also known as 'little willies' made using
a combination of barley and soft wheat flour and rolled into tiny sausages
using 'Lu Ferro'. This is a wire 30cm in length that is used to manipulate and
roll the pasta. I used to use Nonna Carmela's *ferro*, which is seventy years
old. It's now been passed down to my mum, Solidea. I await the honour
of receiving it one lucky day, but until then, I use a piece of an old wired
coathanger. A long wooden skewer would also suffice.

————

Preparation time 1 hour
Cooking time 15 minutes
Serves 4

————

FOR THE PASTA DOUGH
250g barley flour
150g '00' flour
500ml hot water

FOR THE SAUCE
4 tbsp olive oil
2 garlic cloves, peeled and finely sliced
4 large tomatoes, roughly chopped
Pinch of chilli flakes
1.5kg mixed clams, mussels, sliced
    calamari, sliced octopus (including
    tentacles), cleaned
100ml white wine
Salt and pepper to season
Small bunch of parsley, roughly chopped

1 Start by making the pasta. Due to the ratio of barley flour to soft wheat
flour this pasta is a little difficult to work with as it has a tendency to
crumble. The secret is to keep working it by hand and just persevere.
2 Pour both flours onto a wooden board and mix with your hand to
combine. Make a well in the centre and slowly add a little water. Begin to
combine the flour, using a fork or your fingertips if preferred, into the water,
working inside the well.
3 Add more water as required until all of the flour has been combined into
a workable dough.
4 Knead the dough for around 8 minutes until smooth. If the dough is a
little dry, add a little more water. Cover and allow to rest for 30 minutes.
5 Take the dough and cut it in half so it is more manageable to work with.
Cover one half in cling film and set aside until required.
6 Roll the dough into a large sausage then continue to roll it into thin
sausages.
7 Cut acorn-sized pieces of dough off the sausage. Place the *ferro* onto the
top corner of the dough and roll it vigorously forming a sausage with
a hole that runs through the centre.
8 Repeat with the remaining dough.
9 Lay the *minchiareddhi* onto trays. Allow them to dry for 1 hour
before cooking.
10 Place a large pan of water on to boil. Once boiling, salt well then add
the pasta and cook until *al dente*.
11 Pour the olive oil into a large shallow pan and add the garlic. Fry lightly
over a low heat for 2 minutes.
12 Tumble in the tomatoes and chilli flakes. Cook down for 5 minutes on
a medium heat.

CARMELA'S TIPS

Minchiareddhi are also delicious with a heavy tomato sauce and lots of *ricotta scante (forte)*. This pasta is normally made with 80 per cent barley and a 20 per cent '00' flour combination. However, I think the mix I've used in my recipe works better, is easier to handle and doesn't break up when boiled.

13 Add the seafood, white wine, salt, pepper and half the parsley. Stir and clamp on a lid for 4 minutes until all of the mussel and clam shells have opened. Taste for seasoning.

14 Drain the pasta, reserving a ladle of pasta water.

15 Add the pasta to the seafood pan along with reserved water and stir really well.

16 Spoon out into bowls or onto a large platter and enjoy.

STRASCINATI PASTA WITH WILD ROCKET AND TOMATOES

STRASCINATI AL RUCOLA E POMODORI

Strascinati means in essence 'to drag' or a pasta that has been dragged. This may sound a little odd, but I personally find *strascinati* very simple to make. It's basically a flat *orecchiette* that has been dragged across a wooden board with a blunt knife and a thumb (see page 174 for a photo). For those of us that find making the perfect *orecchiette* an almost impossible challenge (I do) I feel somewhat redeemed as *strascinati* are far easier. Served in a classic fresh sweet tomato sauce with lots of peppery wild rocket, both the tomato and rocket complement the pasta beautifully.

Preparation time 10 minutes
Cooking time 25 minutes
Serves 4

400g *strascinati* pasta
3 tbsp olive oil
2 cloves of garlic, peeled and crushed
20 cherry or baby plum tomatoes, halved
3 tomato vines
1 small Parmesan rind
Salt and pepper to season
800g wild rocket, washed
Small handful of fresh basil, torn
Pinch of dried chilli
Pinch of dried oregano or 1 tsp of
    fresh leaves
2 tbsp extra virgin olive oil, to drizzle
100g Parmesan, grated

---

1 Cook the pasta according to the packet instructions in salted boiling water until *al dente*.

2 Meanwhile, pour the olive oil into a sauté pan and gently cook the garlic, stirring, for 2 minutes.

3 Tumble in the tomatoes, vines and the Parmesan rind. Allow the tomatoes to cook down with the rind for 5–7 minutes.

4 Blanch the rocket in a little hot water for 5 minutes. Drain and squeeze out as much excess water as possible.

5 Add the rocket to the tomatoes and stir. Season with salt, pepper and a little chilli and oregano. Cook for 10 minutes on a gentle heat and then remove the tomato vines.

4 Once the pasta is *al dente*, drain it (reserving a small ladle of cooking water). Add the pasta and the cooking water to the rocket along with the basil, then stir to combine.

5 Serve in a bowl with an additional drizzle of extra virgin olive oil and a generous sprinkling of Parmesan.

CARMELA'S TIPS

You can easily substitute the *strascinati* pasta for *orecchiette* or *cavatelli*, if preferred. Out of season, I replace fresh plum tomatoes with tinned.

ORECCHIETTE WITH TURNIP TOPS
ORECCHIETTE CON CIME DI RAPE

Orecchiette is the popular regional pasta of Puglia. Little cap-shaped shells also known as 'little ears', this pasta shape is a tricky one to master; much skill and immense patience is required. Many years of experience with a wooden board and blunt knife will aid you in your quest for the perfect *orecchiette*. I, however, am happy that we are able to buy them relatively easily in my local Italian deli.

Preparation time 15 minutes
Cooking time 20 minutes
Serves 4

_____

500g *orecchiette*, freshly made (page 28)
   or dried
3 tbsp olive oil
2 garlic cloves, peeled and sliced
Salt and pepper to season
1.5kg tender turnip tops (*cime di rape*),
   washed and trimmed
Pinch of dried chilli
Small bunch of basil, torn
100g Parmesan, grated

1 Cook the pasta in salted boiling water according to the packet instructions ensuring it is left with a bite (*al dente*).
2 Meanwhile, blanch the prepared turnip tops for 5 minutes in a large pan of water. Drain the tops then place onto a clean tea towel and squeeze out excess water.
3 Pour the olive oil into a frying pan and gently cook the garlic, stirring, for 2 minutes.
3 Tumble the trimmed turnip tops in with the garlic and stir. Season with salt, pepper and a little chilli. Add half the basil cook for 7 minutes on a gentle heat.
4 Once the pasta is *al dente*, drain it (reserving a small ladle of cooking water). Add the pasta and the reserved cooking water to the turnip tops, then stir to combine.
5 Serve in a bowl with a generous sprinkling of Parmesan and the remaining basil leaves.

CARMELA'S TIP
If turnip tops are hard to come by I often use either cavolo nero, kale or purple sprouting broccoli. Liguria also has its own version of *orecchiette* known as *sugeli*.

SARDINIA

Sardinia is the second largest island in the Mediterranean after Sicily, with Cagliari as its capital. It's a beautiful island – I would even go as far as to say the jewel of the Mediterranean – rugged and hilly and possibly a little barren inland, but as soon as you tiptoe towards the luscious coastline you feel an immediate change. This island stands alone from Italy not only for language but with regards to food, culture, work and history. Sardinians are very proud of their island and consider themselves 'Sardi' rather than Italians.

Sardinia is one of my favourite regions to write about when it comes to pasta, as the style of making pasta here is so different. From *filindeu*, from the town of Nuoro, also knowns as 'God's yarn'– thin strips of pasta stretched over the base of a circular flat basket, an art in itself and only made by a few ladies on the island – to *fregola* a delicate yet robust toasted pasta, voluptuous *culurgiones* filled with potato and mint, *lorighittas* that resemble small ropes, and *malloreddus*, little Sardinian gnocchi, there's so much to discover. I hope you are ready to experience something new and a little different.

▲ Sardinian ravioli combine potatoes and pasta but are still delightfully delicate. (See page 192 for the full recipe.)

▶ Bronze Age Nuraghi ruins – Su Nuraxi di Barumini – are preserved on the beautiful, unspoilt island of Sardinia.

FREGOLA WITH CLAMS AND CHERRY TOMATOES

FREGOLA CON VONGOLE E POMODORINI

Fregola is a delicate yet small coarse pasta from Sardinia that was originally made by hand using semolina flour and water. The pasta mix would be rubbed together to form small peppercorn-sized balls of dough, which would then be dried slowly and toasted to develop the nutty flavour. *Fregola* is available in a range of sizes from fine to medium and coarse. It is one of the shapes I fell in love with instantly as I find it complements so many dishes. Here I have paired it with sweet clams but it's equally delicious in soups with beans and potatoes, and salads too. Search out *fregola* in your local Italian deli.

—————

Preparation time 10 minutes
Cooking time 20 minutes
Serves 4

—————

400g *fregola*
900g small fresh clams in shells
4 tbsp olive oil
2 garlic cloves, peeled and finely chopped
1 small chilli, deseeded and finely chopped
1 x 400g tin cherry tomatoes or 20 cherry tomatoes, halved
Salt and pepper to season
Small bunch of parsley, chopped

1 Place a large pan of water on to boil for the *fregola*, salting the water well once boiling.

2 Wash and clean the clams well in cold water. Ensure all clams are closed and discard any with broken, damaged shells or any that are opened.

3 Put the clams into a large shallow pan. Clamp on a lid and shake well. Allow the clams to cook until all of the tiny clams have opened, approximately 6–7 minutes. Any clams that have not opened should be thrown away. Remove half the clams from the shells, leaving the remainder still with their shells on. Set aside.

4 Heat the oil in a large frying pan and add the chopped garlic and chilli. Cook gently for 4 minutes on a medium heat. Drain the tinned tomatoes through a sieve to remove any excess liquid. Add the sieved tomatoes, or chopped cherry tomatoes if preferred and in season, to the garlic and stir.

5 Cook for 20 minutes, season well with salt and black pepper. Add half the parsley and stir.

6 Add the clams to the tomato sauce and stir.

7 Cook the *fregola* according to the packet instructions, minus 2 minutes to ensure the pasta remains al *dente*.

8 Drain the *fregola* and add to the clams and tomatoes and stir through. Add the remaining parsley and serve.

CARMELA'S TIPS

When using fresh vine tomatoes, add the tomato vines (green stalks) to the sauce, too; they are full of aroma and flavour. Cook the sauce as usual then simply discard the vines. Next time you buy fresh tomatoes, I set you a small task. Smell the tomatoes you are buying complete with vine, then remove the vine and smell the tomatoes again. The aroma will be different as most of it comes from within the vine!

GNOCCHETTI SARDI WITH SAUSAGES AND TOMATO

MALLOREDDUS ALLA CAMPIDANESE

It's back to basics, with *malloreddus* made using *semola rimacinata di grano duno* (semolina flour) and hot water, such a pleasing pasta to make by hand. The ridged (*rigate*) exterior of these delicate shells is simply made for catching the sauce. This is one pasta shape I adore making with my children – a ball of dough and wooden gnocchi board or butter pats are all you need, along with a little patience. This is a traditional recipe paired with the finest Italian sausages and tomatoes.

Preparation time 10 minutes
Cooking time 40 minutes
Serves 4

400g prepared *malloreddus* (page 24) or use dried *gnocchetti sardi*
4 tbsp olive oil
1 large onion, peeled and finely chopped
2 garlic cloves, peeled and crushed
1 small sprig of rosemary, finely chopped
500g Italian sausage, casings removed and roughly chopped
2 x 400g tins plum tomatoes
1 tbsp tomato purée
Small pinch of saffron
150ml vegetable stock, infused with 1g saffron
Large bunch of basil, roughly torn
Salt and pepper to season
90g Sardinian pecorino, grated

1 Place a large pan of water on to boil for the *malloreddus*, salting the water well once boiling.

2 Pour the oil into a large sauté pan and add the chopped onion and garlic. Fry gently on a medium heat, stirring with a wooden spoon for 5 minutes until soft and translucent.

3 Sprinkle in the rosemary and tumble in the sausages (without casings) and stir, breaking up the sausage a little with the back of a wooden spoon. Cook for 10 minutes.

4 Pour in the tinned tomatoes and break them up gently with the wooden spoon. Squeeze in the tomato purée and add the saffron and stock.

5 Stir and add the basil then season with salt and pepper. Cook for a further 25 minutes over a medium heat.

6 Add the *malloreddus* to the pan of boiling salted water and cook until *al dente*, approximately 10 minutes.

7 Drain and tumble the *malloreddus* into the sauce and add a small ladle of pasta water if required.

8 Taste and season. Stir well, then ladle into warm bowls with a generous scattering of grated Sardinian pecorino.

CARMELA'S TIPS
If you have any spare Parmesan or pecorino rinds in your fridge, add one to the sauce for the last 25 minutes of cooking. For a gluten-free version, combine 800g mashed potato with 100g chestnut flour, 1 egg and a pinch of salt. Combine and roll into long thin sausages, cut into 2cm pieces and roll down a gnocchi board.

LORIGHITTAS WITH MIXED SEAFOOD

LORIGHITTAS AI FRUTTI DI MARE

This pasta looks like small rope-like rings and resemble the iron rings that were once fixed outside local Sardinian houses to tether the farmer's horses to. *Lorighittas* are produced in the small village of Morgongiori in a tradition that has been passed down with great pride to the younger generations for many years. The dough is formed into a spaghetti and turned round two fingers and then twisted into each other to gain the rope effect. Although served traditionally with tomatoes, chicken and bay leaves, I have taken my inspiration from the coastline with this recipe. *Lorighittas* are relatively easy to make but it will take time and patience to master the perfect ring by hand.

Preparation time 1 hour 30 minutes
Cooking time 15 minutes
Serves 4

————

400g freshly prepared *lorighittas* (page 27) or dried
4 tbsp olive oil
1 banana shallot, peeled and finely chopped
1 garlic clove, peeled and crushed
8 baby squid, cleaned and cut into 2cm rings, with tentacles
6 scallops, sliced into 4mm slices
8 prawns, shells intact, gut track removed
Small bunch of parsley, chopped
Pinch of chilli (optional)
Salt and pepper to season
1 lemon, cut into wedges

————

1 Place a large pan of water on to boil for the *lorighittas*, salting the water well once boiling.
2 Add the *lorighittas* to the pan and cook for 10 minutes if freshly made, or follow the packet instructions, minus 2 minutes, if they are dried. Drain, reserving a ladle of the water, and set aside.
3 Pour the olive oil into a large shallow pan and add the shallots and garlic. Cook over a low heat, stirring gently, until translucent.
4 Add the squid, tentacles, scallops and prawns to the garlic and shallots in the pan. Stir and season with salt and pepper. Cook for 3 minutes. Add a pinch of chilli if desired.
5 Add the cooked pasta to the pan with a small ladle of pasta water and stir. The pasta water will help to emulsify the light sauce. Keep stirring and scatter in the parsley. Check for seasoning.
6 Spoon into warm bowls, making sure everyone receives two prawns each, nestled on top of the pasta. Serve with lemon wedges.

SARDINIAN RAVIOLI WITH POTATO, BURNT BUTTER AND SAGE

CULURGIONES CON BURRO E SALVIA

Culurgiones, culingionis, culurzones... The famous Sardinian filled pasta with so many names. Are you ready for a delicate pasta stuffed with potato? The combination is perfect. These filled *culurgiones* are voluptuous and when handmade are incredibly decorative too, resembling an ear of wheat (see page 184 for a photo). It has taken me a long time to master this seemingly easy yet tricky shape. I have paired them here with a simple sage and butter sauce, but a tomato sauce would work equally well. Change the sauce depending on the filling.

Preparation time 1 hour
(plus resting time)
Cooking time 30 minutes
Serves 4

FOR THE PASTA DOUGH

400g semolina flour
   (*semola di grano duro*)
200ml hot water

FOR THE FILLING

600g Maris Piper potatoes
5 mint leaves, shredded very finely
150g Sardinian pecorino, grated
1 large whole egg plus a yolk
1 garlic clove, peeled and crushed
Pinch of freshly grated nutmeg
Salt and pepper to season

FOR THE SAUCE

200g butter
4 sage leaves
Squeeze of lemon juice
Small handful of parsley and basil,
   finely chopped
30g Sardinian pecorino, grated, to finish

CARMELA'S TIPS
The *culurgiones* can be made up to
48 hours in advance.

1 Start by making the filling. Boil the potatoes with their skins on (to prevent them absorbing water and becoming wet) in a large pan of water.

2 When the potatoes are cooked through, drain and allow to cool for 15 minutes or until you can bear to peel them.

3 Peel the potatoes and put through a potato ricer. The ricer ensures a smooth and even mash.

4 Place the riced potatoes in a bowl and add the remaining filling ingredients. Stir and cover. Place in the fridge until required.

5 Make the pasta as described on page 24, cover and allow to rest for 30 minutes.

6 Roll the pasta out by hand with a rolling pin or using a pasta machine, to a thickness of 3mm.

7 Cut out 7cm rounds using a cutter.

8 Transfer the potato mixture to a piping bag and secure the top.

9 Make a small slit at the bottom of the bag.

10 Holding the piping bag, pipe a small sausage of potato onto the centre of the pasta.

11 Fold the bottom of the dough up onto the potato filling and start pinching the dough from each side to the other, keeping the pleats small and tight, to form an ear of wheat. Squeeze any excess filling out and pinch the end to seal.

12 Continue in the same way with the remaining pasta.

13 Bring a large pan of water to boil. When boiling, salt well, add the *culurgiones* and cook for 4–5 minutes.

14 Meanwhile, place the butter and sage in a shallow pan over a medium heat. Allow the butter to turn golden. Add a spritz of lemon juice, the parsley and basil. Stir.

15 Using a slotted spoon, add the *culurgiones* to the butter. Serve with an additional grating of pecorino.

SPAGHETTI WITH GRATED FISH ROE
SPAGHETTI ALLA BOTTARGA

Bottarga, a dry cured salted fish roe of mullet, tuna or ling, is loved by Sardinians and used liberally in Sardinian cooking. Grated over a simple crostini, sliced and marinated in oil and lemon juice or grated over freshly made pasta to finish, *bottarga* offers a salty taste of the sea and is one of those products that adds an instant depth of flavour and aroma to a simple bowl of pasta. It is available in good Italian delis and keeps well in the fridge, too.

————

Preparation time 5 minutes
Cooking time 15 minutes
Serves 4

————

400g dried spaghetti
80g *bottarga*
80g unsalted butter
2 tbsp extra virgin olive oil
Salt and pepper to season
Small bunch or parsley, finely chopped

1 Place a large pan of water on to boil for the spaghetti. Salt the water well when boiling and cook the spaghetti according to the packet instructions, minus 2 minutes, to ensure it is left with a bite (*al dente*).
2 Into a sauté pan, add the butter and oil and warm gently.
3 Add 60g of the *bottarga* in thin slices to the butter and season with a little salt and good grind of black pepper. Stir and allow the *bottarga* to heat gently for 5 minutes.
4 Drain the pasta, reserving 30ml of the water. Add the spaghetti to the *bottarga*, along with the reserved pasta water to help emulsify the sauce.
5 Sprinkle in the parsley and stir.
6 Serve in bowls with an additional grating of the remaining *bottarga*.

CARMELA'S TIPS
Mario Olianas, one of my good friends from Sardinia, is now based in Leeds and makes his own *bottarga* from either silver mullet or cod roe. Amazing!

————

SICILY

SICILIA

La bella Sicilia, known for the silent echo and rumble of Mount Etna, the famous sweet-tasting Marsala wine (in which I love to dip *cantucci*, almond biscotti), beautiful colourful countryside, bustling fishing ports and stunning churches and palaces. Sicily is the largest island in the Mediterranean, with Palermo standing proud as its capital.

▲ Fresh fruit and vegetables for sale in Ballaro, a famous market in Palermo, Sicily.

▶ Moorish influences can be seen in the decorarive architecture as well as the food of Sicily.

Influences from the Middle East and North Africa were welcomed into the kitchen of most Sicilian homes many years ago. A huge variety of spice and dried fruit have been embraced – from citrus fruits, dried fruits and nuts to herbs and spices such as saffron, cumin, cinnamon and sumac. The knowledge and passion the cooks of Sicily bring to something like using cinnamon in pasta and sultanas in meatballs brings a smile to my face.

I have included some of my favourite recipes in this chapter, using fresh vegetables and beautiful fish and seafood. A fabulous range of pasta shapes and techniques, too, have come from Sicily. From much-loved *ziti* pasta, twisted *busiate*, pasta pie made with tiny hoop-earring-shaped pasta, and handmade irregular couscous created using a regional steam pot called a *cuscusera*.

ANELLETTI PASTA PIE

TIMBALLO DI ANELLETTI

I love the term 'pasta pie'. It reminds me of the Dean Martin song 'That's Amore', where he sang about pizza pie and *pasta e fazzol*; it's a song that encompasses everything Italian, including the vital elements of love and food. *Anelletti* are small hoop-earring shapes, delicious in soups, but here they are embraced with a rich tomato and pea sauce and baked. This dish is said to come from the province of Palermo.

———

Preparation time 25 minutes
Cooking time 2 hours 30 minutes
Serves 4

———

450g anelletti pasta
3 tbsp olive oil
1 small onion, peeled and finely chopped
1 carrot, peeled and finely chopped
1 stick celery, finely chopped
2 garlic cloves, peeled and crushed
200g beef mince
200g veal mince
200g pork mince
200ml red wine
1 tbsp tomato purée
200g peas, shelled, or frozen
1 x 680g bottle passata
1 x 400g tin chopped tomatoes
Small bunch of celery leaves,
    finely chopped
1 bay leaf
A few marjoram leaves
10 basil leaves
Salt and pepper to season
1 tbsp butter
3 tbsp breadcrumbs, lightly toasted
200g *caciocavallo* (firm Italian cheese)
125g mozzarella
60g Parmesan or pecorino

CARMELA'S TIPS

I often add chopped boiled eggs into the pasta pie for added texture and flavour – and just because I love eggs. If you are unable to find *caciocavallo* cheese, provolone is a good alternative.

———

1 Into a large saucepan, add the olive oil followed by the onion, carrot and celery. Cook gently over a medium heat for around 5 minutes until softened.

2 Add the garlic, cook for an additional 2 minutes and stir.

3 Add all the mince to the pan and colour completely.

4 Squeeze the tomato purée into the red wine and stir.

5 Add the red wine to the mince, stir and allow the wine to evaporate, about 4 minutes.

6 Tumble in the peas (I use frozen peas straight from the freezer).

7 Pour the passata and tinned tomatoes into the mince along with the celery leaves, bay leaf, marjoram and basil. Stir and season with salt and pepper.

8 Allow the sugo (sauce) to cook over a medium to low heat for 2 hours, stirring occasionally, and check intermittently for seasoning.

9 Preheat the oven to 180°C (gas 4).

10 Bring a large pan of water to the boil. When boiling, salt well, add the *anelletti* and cook as per packet instructions, minus 4 minutes, as you will be baking this dish.

11 Butter a medium bakeware dish or pre-sprung cake tin (23cm diameter x 5cm height).

12 Sprinkle the toasted breadcrumbs into the buttered dish, covering the base and sides.

13 Remove the bay leaf from the sauce.

14 Drain the pasta. Tip the pasta back into the saucepan, add two ladles of the sauce. and stir. Ladle a layer of pasta into the dish or tin, sprinkle over a mixture of the cheeses then add another ladle of sauce.

15 Repeat until the dish is full and you have used up all of the sauce, finishing the top with sauce and cheese.

16 Bake for 30 minutes. If you have baked the pasta pie in a bakeware dish, then simply serve, but if you have use a sprung tin you should be able to turn it out gently.

HOW TO MAKE FRESH COUSCOUS BY HAND

All you need is a little time, together with semolina flour and water. Yet again, two ingredients make the most fantastic start to a very simple dish. You will need a *maffaradda*, a traditional earthenware dish that has small holes in the base, which would be placed over a pan of boiling water or stock. Alternatively, a colander with a muslin laid inside it would suffice, propped over a pan of boiling water.

Makes 6 servings

FOR THE COUSCOUS
400g coarse semolina flour
(*semola di grano duro*)
Water, to bind

FOR THE DOUGH SEAL
200g semolina flour
100ml water

———

1 For the couscous, pour the semolina into a large shallow dish.

2 It's important not to add too much water to the semolina flour and to work very lightly with your fingers. I tend to add a few tablespoons of water at a time and gently stir the semolina with my fingertips, in a similar way to making a crumble topping. Add more water as required and work the grains gently until they turn into small irregular balls or pellets of couscous.

3 Place a clean tea towel on a table and tumble out the couscous. Level out with your fingertips.

4 The couscous is steamed in a traditional way over a hob. The couscous would be seasoned with garlic, onion and parsley and stirred or as above, just a little saffron would be added.

5 Place the couscous in a *maffaradda*. I normally line it with a muslin sheet because even though the holes are small my couscous is still able to disappear through them.

6 To form a dough seal, mix 200g semolina flour and 100ml of water together. Form the dough into a sausage and place it around the bottom of the *maffaradda* at the top of the pan of water, to prevent any steam escaping.

7 Place a damp cloth over the *maffaradda*, making sure there are no gaps.

8 Allow the couscous to steam for 1 hour to 1 hour 15 minutes.

9 Once cooked, fork through and finish off with your chosen sauce.

COASTAL TRAPANI FISH COUSCOUS

CUSCUSU DI TRAPANI

Sicily is an enchanted island, where Middle Eastern influences are still very much cherished. This couscous can be made by hand in a bowl called a *maffaradda*, but I think nowadays most families use the pre-made variety for speed, traditionally serving it with a fish stock and coastal mixed fish. If time is on your side, however, have a go at making the couscous yourself (page 198).

Preparation time 15 minutes
Cooking time 45 minutes
Serves 4

Generous pinch of saffron
4 tbsp olive oil
1 red onion, peeled and finely chopped
1 stick celery with leaves, finely chopped
1 medium carrot, peeled and
    finely chopped
3 garlic cloves, peeled and finely sliced
Handful of parsley, chopped (reserve
    some to sprinkle)
500g tomatoes, peeled and roughly
    chopped
1 tbsp tomato purée
Pinch of dried chilli flakes (optional)
Salt and pepper, season to taste
1 bay leaf
1kg mixed fish, cleaned and gutted
    (with heads on to add flavour): red
    mullet, John Dory, snapper, octopus,
    eel, clams, mussels, choose your
    favourite combination
150ml fish stock
15 saffron strands
400g couscous, pre-prepared (page 198)
    or ready-made
½ tsp cinnamon
Sprinkle of freshly grated nutmeg
30g almonds, blanched, roughly chopped

1 Pour the oil into a large shallow sauté pan. Add the onion, celery, carrot and garlic. Fry gently over a medium heat for 5 minutes.

2 Add half the parsley and stir.

3 Spoon in the tomato pulp and tomato purée, stir and sprinkle in the chilli if using. Cook for a further 10 minutes. Season with salt and pepper and lay the bay leaf on top of the tomatoes.

4 Add the mixed fish to the pan. Try and keep them in a single layer if possible.

5 Ladle in the fish stock and clamp on the lid and cook for 20 minutes. Halfway through cooking I normally flip the fish gently.

6 Once the fish is cooked through, remove it from the pan. Allow the fish to cook slightly off the heat. Using your fingers, remove all of the tender fish from the bones and set aside.

7 Discard the bay leaf.

8 Add the saffron strands to a little boiling water to help to awaken the spice.

9 Place 400g of couscous into a bowl and pour in 600ml of boiling water and the saffron strands. Stir and cover with cling film for 10 minutes.

10 Once the couscous is ready, break up the grains with a fork. Sprinkle in the cinnamon and grate in a little fresh nutmeg. Stir well. Add 2 tablespoons extra virgin olive oil and fork through again. Check the couscous for seasoning.

11 Add half the fish sauce from the pan to the couscous and stir.

12 Transfer the couscous to a large platter.

13 Return the flaked fish to the remaining sauce, stir and spoon over the couscous.

14 Sprinkle over a little reserved chopped parsley and almonds.

PASTA WITH AUBERGINE

PASTA ALLA NORMA

Without a doubt, this recipe is a Sicilian classic: plump aubergine paired with tomatoes and a short pasta. I still salt my aubergines; I find this step an essential in removing excess water and bitterness. Add some chilli if you like a little heat.

---

1 Top and tail the aubergines and cut into small cubes.

2 Place the aubergine cubes into a colander and salt well with the coarse salt. Place a plate on top to weigh the cubes down and allow to drain for at least an hour.

3 Heat 1 tablespoon of olive oil in a saucepan, add the shallot and garlic. Fry gently for around 5 minutes until translucent but not coloured.

4 Add the tomatoes and stir. Using the back of a wooden spoon, break up the tomatoes.

5 Season with salt and pepper and cook for 15 minutes.

6 Lightly rinse off the salt from the cubed aubergines and squeeze gently between some kitchen towels to remove any excess water.

7 In a frying pan, heat the olive oil and fry off the aubergine cubes until they are lightly coloured. Drain on kitchen towel to remove excess oil and add to the tomato sauce. Cook for a further 15 minutes.

8 Add the basil and check for seasoning.

9 Cook your pasta in salted water according to the packet instructions, minus 2 minutes to ensure it remains *al dente*. Drain the pasta and add to the tomato sauce, reserving a ladle of the pasta water. Add a little of the reserved water to loosen the sauce. Sprinkle in the *ricotta salata*, stir and serve.

Preparation time 1 hour 15 minutes
Cooking time 30 minutes
Serves 4

400g *busiati* or *maccheroni*
1 large or 2 small aubergines
Coarse salt (for sprinkling over
   the aubergines)
Olive oil, for frying
1 shallot, peeled and sliced
2 garlic cloves, peeled and crushed
2 x 340g tins plum tomatoes
Salt and pepper to season
100g *ricotta salata* (salted ricotta)
Small handful of basil, torn

BUSIATE WITH PESTO TRAPANESE

BUSIATE AL PESTO TRAPANESE

Warming sunshine in a bowl – the Sicilians pride themselves on their fresh tomato and almond pesto. This is an alternative to the pesto you are probably familiar with, pesto *Genovese* from Genoa. Pesto *trapanese* is from and named after the province of Trapani on the west coast of Sicily. I tend to make this pesto in a food processor for speed; however, if you prefer to keep with rustic tradition use a pestle and mortar.

Preparation time 10 minutes
Cooking time 12 minutes
Serves 4

400g *busiati* or *casarrece*
100g whole almonds, peeled, blanched
500g fresh plum ripe tomatoes, quartered
3 garlic cloves, peeled
Pinch of dried chilli (optional)
Small bunch of basil
80g Parmesan
50ml extra virgin olive oil
Salt, pepper to season

FOR THE TOPPING
80g toasted breadcrumbs
Small bunch of basil

1 Place a large pan of water on to boil for the pasta. Once boiling, salt the water well and cook the pasta until it is *al dente*.
2 Put 80g of the almonds, the tomatoes, garlic cloves, chilli, if using, basil and Parmesan into a food processor and blitz until you have a rough texture.
3 Pour in half the oil and blitz again. Season with salt and pepper and taste.
4 Add the remaining oil gradually until you have a dropping consistency.
5 To make a topping, blitz the breadcrumbs and the basil in a food processor for 30 seconds.
6 Drain the pasta and reserve 20ml of pasta water.
7 Tumble the pasta into a large bowl along with the reserved pasta water.
8 Spoon in all of the pesto and stir to combine.
9 Sprinkle over the flavoured breadcrumbs and add a chopped scattering of the remaining almonds.

ZITI WITH SARDINES, CHICORY AND BREADCRUMBS

ZITI CON SARDE, CICORIA E PANGRATTATO

This is a truly Sicilian dish that takes its influences from the Middle East. With a small mouthful of this pasta dish you will feel the warmth of the sun on your back and get a taste of how diverse Sicily as a region really is. *Ziti* pasta comes in many sizes, from a small *maccheroni* to the length of a spaghetti, but it is more of a tube than a strand. It's a versatile pasta that's great to have in your storecupboard.

———

Preparation time 15 minutes
Cooking time 40 minutes
Serves 4

———

400g short *ziti*
5 tbsp olive oil
140g slightly stale breadcrumbs
1 medium onion, peeled and chopped
1 garlic clove, peeled and sliced
60g pine nuts
70g raisins, soaked in a little stock
4 anchovy fillets, washed and chopped
1 x 680g bottle passata
200ml water
350g fresh sardines, cleaned and chopped into bite-sized pieces
280g chicory, washed and chopped
Small pinch of saffron (soaked in a little stock)
Salt and pepper to season
Small bunch of basil leaves, chopped
Small bunch of parsley, chopped

1 In a frying pan, heat 2 tablespoons of oil and add the breadcrumbs. Lightly toast the breadcrumbs for around 4 minutes until lightly golden. Once ready, take them off the heat and set aside.

2 Add the remaining oil to a sauté pan and cook the onion and garlic over a medium heat for 5 minutes until transparent.

3 Add the pine nuts to the pan and stir. Keep a beady eye on the pine nuts as they can burn and scorch very easily.

4 Drain the raisins and add them to the pan along with the anchovy fillets and stir. Cook for 3 minutes then add the passata and water.

5 Roughly chop the sardines and add them to the passata along with the chicory. Add the saffron with the stock, stir and cook over a gentle simmer for 20 minutes.

6 Season with salt and pepper.

7 Mix the chopped basil with the cooled toasted breadcrumbs.

8 Place a large pan of water on to boil and add the *ziti*. Cook the pasta according to the packet instructions, minus 2 minutes to ensure the pasta remains *al dente*.

9 Drain the ziti and reserve a small ladle of pasta water.

10 Add the reserved pasta water and *ziti* to the sauce and stir. Tumble in the parsley.

11 Serve in warm bowls with a generous scattering of toasted breadcrumbs.

TRENTINO-ALTO ADIGE

The cooking in this region of northern Italy is influenced greatly by many other cuisines – Germany, France, Austria and, of course, a delicious Italian combination. The Dolomites form the peak of this region, with Trento as its capital. It's a region that would be any mountain lover's idea of paradise: idyllic with a touch of charm. The capital houses many beer halls and you many even find apple strudel on the menu, an obvious influence from its border with Austria. Cycle lovers can experience the 400-mile cycle path that runs through, as well as stopping off at a vineyard or two.

The recipes I have selected for this region showcase the differences between the north and south of Italy. *Spätzle* extruded through tiny holes and served with a butter drizzle, celestine pancakes served with *brodo*, and plump moist *canederli*, flavoured bread balls served with either stock or butter. I have also given instructions in the pasta-colouring section (page 37) on how to colour pasta using pig's blood. Named *blutnudeln* or *pasta al sangue*, this is a speciality of Pusteria. Different? Absolutely. Moreish? Most definitely.

▶ *Spätzle*, also known and referred to as 'little sparrows', will only be found in Trentino and what a treasure it is.

▶ Vineyards in winter, Trentino. The food from this region is as different from that of the south as the landscape and climate are.

BREAD DUMPLINGS WITH SPECK AND SALAMI

CANEDERLI DI SPECK E SALUMI IN BRODO

When I think of Trentino-Alto Adige I immediately think of beautiful plump *canederli*. They remind me very much of my *polpette* from Puglia, but they have a slightly more comforting feel to them. There are many variations, from those based more on a cheese flavour to delicious liver *candereli*. To lighten the *canederli* you can also add a quarter teaspoon of bicarbonate of soda. Served in stock or with melted butter, these are a must for any dinner table.

Preparation time 30 minutes
Cooking time 20 minutes
Serves 4

600g stale bread, cut into tiny cubes
370ml milk
100g speck or Parma ham , finely sliced
50g salami, roughly sliced
1 garlic clove, peeled and crushed
2 tbsp chives, finely chopped
4 medium eggs
2 tbsp '00' flour
Salt and pepper to season
1 litre beef stock
60g Parmesan

1 Place the stale bread in a large mixing bowl.
2 Pour over the milk and squish the bread down with the back of a wooden spoon. To allow the bread to absorb the milk a little, leave to stand for 10 minutes.
3 Add the speck, salami and garlic. Stir.
4 Sprinkle in three quarters of the chives and crack in the eggs. Stir to incorporate. Season with salt and pepper.
5 Add the flour to bind the mixture.
6 Leave to rest for 15 minutes.
7 Bring the stock up to simmering point.
8 Wet your hands to roll the *canederli* into the size of small satsumas. If you prefer, use two tablespoons and form beautiful quenelles.
9 Drop the rolled and formed *canederli* into the stock and cook for 15–20 minutes.
10 Remove the *canederli* with a slotted spoon, place three per person into bowls. Add a ladle of beef stock and a sprinkle of Parmesan and chives to each.

MEZZALUNE PASTA WITH SPINACH AND RICOTTA

CAJINCI T'EGA

Trentino Alto Adige has to be one of the most diverse regions in Italy, and is becoming one of my favourite regions to cook and eat from. This dish is a simple *mezzaluna* pasta made with a combination of flours; it's delicious and incredibly satisfying. The spinach can easily be replaced with another green, from kale to stewed cavolo nero or even *cime di rape* (turnip tops).

Preparation time 1 hour
Cooking time 10 minutes
Serves 4

FOR THE PASTA DOUGH
350g spelt wholemeal flour
150g '00' flour
3 large eggs
100ml milk, tepid
Polenta or semolina, for dusting

FOR THE FILLING
350g spinach, blanched,
   squeezed and puréed
800g ricotta
90g Parmesan, grated
1 egg yolk
½ nutmeg, freshly grated
Salt and pepper to season

FOR THE SAUCE
80g butter
Small bunch of chives, finely chopped
80g Parmesan, grated

1 Combine both flours and tip them onto a large wooden board.

2 Whisk the eggs and the tepid milk together.

3 Make a well in the centre of the flour and pour the wet ingredients in gradually. Begin to combine using a fork.

4 Form into a dough and knead for 5–7 minutes until smooth and elastic.

5 Wrap the dough in cling film and set aside for a minimum of 30 minutes.

6 To make the filling, blitz the spinach until smooth. Scrape into a bowl along with the ricotta, Parmesan, egg yolk, nutmeg, salt and pepper. Stir well. Taste the mixture and check for additional seasoning.

7 For ease, spoon the mixture into a disposable piping bag, or simply cover in the bowl and chill while you prepare the pasta.

8 Take the rested pasta dough and cut it in half. Whilst working with one half, ensure you cover the other half so it doesn't dry out and form a skin.

9 Flour the dough and pat it down into a disc. Using a pasta machine, roll through the first setting.

10 'Envelope-fold' the dough into three and roll again. Repeat this six times on the widest setting. This will ensure a smooth, elastic dough.

11 Now run the dough twice through each setting without any folding. I tend to not use the last setting as I find it makes the pasta too thin. You can also roll the pasta with a rolling pin to the thickness of a lasagne sheet.

12 Cut 6cm circles out of the dough using a pastry cutter. Pipe or spoon large teaspoonfuls of the filling onto the centre of each disc.

13 Dampen the circumference of the discs and fold the pasta over, removing excess air and securing into delicate half-moon shapes. Place the finished shapes onto a tray dusted with polenta or semolina. Repeat with the remaining pasta.

14 Place a large pan of water on to boil. Once boiling, salt well and cook the pasta until *al dente*.

15 Melt the butter in a small pan until it turns a light nutty shade of brown.

16 Use a slotted spoon to remove the pasta into warm bowls. Add a drizzle of melted butter, a sprinkle of Parmesan and a scattering of chives.

CELESTINE PASTA PANCAKES IN STOCK

CELESTINE IN BRODO

This is the kind of recipe that I tend to make with my four children. The batter is so easy to prepare, and then of course they get to toss the pasta pancakes far too high into the air. The beef stock can easily be substituted for a chicken or, of course, a delicious vegetable stock.

Preparation and chilling time 40 minutes
Cooking time 30 minutes
Serves 4

200g '00' flour
500ml milk
4 medium eggs
Pinch of salt and twist of pepper
Small bunch each of basil and parsley, finely chopped (save some for the finish)
Olive oil, to fry
1 litre beef stock
80g Parmesan, grated

1 Place the flour in a large bowl.

2 Combine the milk and eggs together in a separate bowl.

3 Slowly whisk the wet ingredients into the dry.

4 Season with salt and pepper. Sprinkle in the finely chopped herbs and stir.

5 Cover the batter with cling film and place in the fridge for 30 minutes to rest.

6 Warm the stock over a low heat while you prepare the pasta pancakes.

7 Pour a dash of oil into a frying pan. Add a small ladleful of the batter and swirl to ensure the batter has coated the bottom of the pan fully. Ensure you keep the pancakes thin. Cook for 2 minutes on each side.

8 Once cooked, transfer the pasta pancake to a plate to cool and repeat until all of the batter is used up.

9 Roll each pancake up into a cylinder and cut into thin slices, similar to the thickness of a fettucine or tagliatelle.

10 Warm the sliced pasta pancakes in the stock and serve with a sprinkle of the reserved herbs and the Parmesan.

ORZO MINESTRONE SOUP

MINESTRA DI ORZO

Soups always go down really well around our family dinner table. I think this is mainly because they are easy to eat – no real effort is required, only lifting of a spoon and, of course, dipping of the bread. *Orzo* pasta is now widely available in many supermarkets and Italian delis. *Orzo* resembles large grains of rice and is incredibly versatile in many dishes. I also use it often simply cooked in stock as I would *pastina*; just before the pasta is cooked I crack in an egg and stir ferociously. Scrumptious.

Preparation time 10 minutes
Cooking time 30 minutes
Serves 4

———

400g *orzo* pasta
1 tbsp olive oil, plus extra to drizzle
25g unsalted butter
250g pancetta, sliced or small cubes
1 garlic clove, peeled and crushed
2 carrots, peeled and cut into tiny cubes
1 celery stick, cut into tiny cubes
1 small leek, cleaned, peeled and
   finely sliced
2 litres of vegetable or chicken stock
2 medium potatoes, peeled and cut
   into small cubes
Small handful of celery leaves, chopped
200g tinned borlotti beans, rinsed in
   cold water
Salt and pepper to season
Parmesan rind (optional)
Few basil leaves, roughly torn
80g Grana Padano, grated

1 Add the olive oil and butter to a deep-sided saucepan. Over a medium heat, lightly fry off the pancetta for 5 minutes.
2 Add the garlic, carrot, celery and leek. Fry for 5 minutes to soften. Stir well.
3 Pour in the stock and stir.
4 Tumble in the potatoes, celery leaves and borlotti beans. Stir and season with salt and pepper.
5 If you have a Parmesan rind I would drop it in now for added flavour.
6 Allow the potatoes to cook for 5 minutes, then add the pasta and stir.
7 Cook the pasta until *al dente*.
8 Scatter the basil into the soup and serve in warm bowls with a sprinkle of Grana Padano and a drizzle of extra virgin olive oil.

SPINACH SPÄTZLE SPARROWS WITH A TALEGGIO DRIZZLE

SPÄTZLE

I just love how Trentino-Alto Adige embraces not only language but some of the culture of its neighbours, too. *Spätzle*, also known and referred to as 'little sparrows', will only be found in this region and what a treasure it is. The mixture is made very loosely and then extruded or pushed through a *spätzle*-maker or press. These are very inexpensive and easy to purchase online, but you can also use a standard kitchen colander. This pasta shape isn't particularly pretty so don't worry about appearance; just embrace the flavour and simplicity.

Preparation time 40 minutes
Cooking time 10 minutes
Serves 4

_____

FOR THE SPÄTZLE
250g spinach, blanched and squeezed
240ml milk
2 medium eggs
650g '00' flour
½ tsp nutmeg, freshly grated
Salt and pepper to season

FOR THE SAUCE
20g butter
100g prosciutto, sliced
150ml single cream
60g taleggio cheese

_____

1 Place the spinach, milk and eggs in a blender and blitz until smooth.
2 Pour the flour into a large bowl and add the nutmeg and a twist of salt and pepper.
3 Scrape the contents of the blender into the flour and stir with a wooden spoon or spatula to incorporate fully. The mixture should be loose, with a dropping consistency.
4 Place a large pan of water on to boil. Once boiling, salt well.
5 Prepare the sauce. In a small skillet melt the butter over a medium heat and sauté the prosciutto for 2 minutes.
6 Pour in the cream. Once the cream has come to a slight simmer add the taleggio and stir with a wooden spoon. Allow the cheese to melt and season with salt and pepper.
7 Take your *spätzle*-maker or colander and push the mixture in batches into the water. When the *spätzle* are cooked, they will float to the top. You may need to cook them in batches.
8 Once cooked, use a slotted spoon to remove them. Serve the *spätzle* in a bowl with a drizzle of the freshly made taleggio sauce.

TUSCANY
TOSCANA

Tuscany, the region of day-dreamers, wine and gastronomic delights. Situated in the centre of Italy, this region has the most stunning landscapes, perfect sunsets and, of course, tantalising food from the Tuscan kitchen. I have visited the region over the past three years as a tourist, as a food writer and as a fellow Italian in search of something off the beaten track. I was overwhelmed by some of the fantastic dishes I came across. Florence is the capital of the region and has a further nine provinces, all echoing a simple yet rustic style of cooking.

Tuscany is regionally rich in truffles, mushrooms, beef, cured meat, vegetables and tender legumes and more, and of course not forgetting the famous unsalted Tuscan bread. Now pasta in the region isn't necessarily abundant but there are a couple of different styles that are worth searching out: *pici* pasta is a thick hand-rolled spaghetti hailing from Siena, along with the pancake-style of pasta named *testaroli*.

▲ Frescoes of Monte Oliveto Maggiore abbey, near Siena, in Tuscany.

▶ Olive trees and vineyards near Volterra, make a typically Tuscan scene.

PICI WITH A PUNGENT GARLIC SAUCE
PICI ALL AGLIONE

Pici are from the beautiful ancient city of Siena in Tuscany, It's simply a chunky, voluptuous spaghetti: beautiful robust rolls of pasta dough made by hand, each one different in size and appearance. Time consuming to make, but worth the effort. So many sauces suit this type of pasta – a dense and rich boar sugo as page 218 (*pici con il ragu di cinghiale*), a duck sauce (*pici con la nana*), or a lighter seasoned stale breadcrumb combination (*pici con le briciole*). There's so much to choose from.

Preparation time 1 hour
Cooking time 30 minutes
Serves 4

FOR THE PASTA
400g semolina flour
   (*semola di grano duro*)
200ml hot water
Polenta, for dusting

FOR THE SAUCE
4 tbsp olive oil
6 garlic cloves, peeled and finely sliced
600g tomato pulp or passata
1 small chilli, deseeded and finely sliced
Small bunch of fresh basil, torn
100g pecorino, grated
Salt and pepper to season

1 Onto a wooden board, tumble the semolina flour. Make a well in the centre of the flour and slowly add half the water.
2 Start working the water into the flour, slowly adding the remaining water. Form a ball of dough and knead for 5 minutes until elastic and smooth to touch.
3 Cover with cling film and allow to rest for a minimum of 30 minutes.
4 Cut the dough in half, cover one half and set aside.
5 Roll the dough out into a rectangle to a thickness of roughly 1cm.
6 Use a sharp knife and cut the dough into long strips 5mm thick.
7 Take each strand and roll into a long sausage, just like a fat spaghetti. Place onto a clean tea towel or onto a tray scattered with a little polenta.
8 Continue with the remaining dough until you have an army of *pici*. Allow the dough to dry for an hour.
9 Pour the olive oil into a saucepan and fry the garlic gently over a medium heat for 5 minutes; do not allow the garlic to colour.
10 Add the tomato pulp or passata and stir. Scatter in the chilli and season with salt and pepper.
11 Cook the sauce for 25 minutes. Five minutes before the sauce is ready add the fresh basil leaves
12 Place a large pan of water on to boil. Once boiling, salt well, add the *pici* and cook until *al dente*.
13 Drain the *pici*, reserving a ladle of pasta water. Tip the *pici* back into the pan and add the tomato sauce and a small amount of the reserved pasta water. Stir and sprinkle through 40g pecorino. Stir and serve in warm bowls with additional pecorino if desired.

CARMELA'S TIPS
If time isn't on your side, use 400g dried *pici* in place of fresh.

PAPPARDELLE WITH A WILD BOAR SAUCE

PAPPARDELLE CON IL RAGU DI CINGHIALE

Pappardelle paired with wild boar ragu: a match made in heaven, as good as sun-blushed tomatoes with a pinch of salt and extra virgin olive oil or even Nutella and warm toasted Italian bread. Pappardelle are a wide flat pasta ribbons measuring approximately 3cm in diameter and the length of spaghetti. This pasta can take a heavy sauce as the sauce grabs and clings beautifully to the strands.

Preparation time 20 minutes
Cooking time 4 hours
Serves 4

400g pappardelle
4 tbsp olive oil
1 celery stick, finely chopped
1 white onion, peeled and finely chopped
1 carrot, peeled and finely chopped
2 cloves garlic, peeled and crushed
Sprig of fresh rosemary
500g wild boar, small chunks
200g Italian sausage, skinned
1 tbsp tomato purée
200ml red wine
600g passata
150ml water
Small bunch of parsley, finely chopped
Small bunch of basil, finely chopped
Salt and pepper to season
80g pecorino, grated

1 Use dried pappardelle or make fresh ones using the same method as you would for tagliatelle (page 38), but just hand cut them to 3cm in width.
2 Pour the oil into a large sauté pan. Over a medium heat, add the celery, onion and carrot. Stir and cook to soften for around 10 minutes.
3 Add the garlic and rosemary sprig. Stir and cook for 2 minutes.
4 Add the wild boar meat and sausage chunks. Sear the meat for 10 minutes, then add the tomato purée and stir.
5 Pour in the red wine, stir and reduce by half.
6 Add the passata, water, all the parsley and half the basil. Stir and season with salt and pepper.
7 Cook over a low heat for 3½ hours. If the sauce looks a little dry, add some chicken stock or water.
8 Place a large pan of water on to boil for the pappardelle. Once boiling, salt well and cook the pappardelle until *al dente*.
9 Add the pasta ribbons to the sauce with the remaining basil and 30g of pecorino. Stir and serve with a dusting of pecorino.

CARMELA'S TIPS
Tagliatelle would work well in this recipe, too.

BADLY MADE PASTA WITH ROCKET AND PANCETTA

MALFATI CON RUCOLA E PANCETTA

Malfati means 'badly made' and in this dish it refers to badly made pasta. However, it's not so much badly made as misshapen, made from scraps of pasta cut into various pieces to eliminate waste. This dish very much echoes *cucina povera* cooking. In this recipe, I use rocket (*rucola*), but as an alternative cavolo nero would work very well too. I also sometimes add some toasted pine nuts to the finished dish.

Preparation time 15 minutes
Cooking time 15 minutes
Serves 4

400g *malfati*, dried or fresh (see tip box)
5 tbsp olive oil
1 medium onion, peeled and
    finely chopped
300g rocket, plus extra leaves to garnish
400g pancetta, cubed
2 garlic cloves, peeled and crushed
1 small chilli, deseeded and finely sliced
Salt and pepper to season
80g pecorino, grated

1 Pour the oil into a sauté pan and add the onion over a medium heat. Stir and cook to soften for 10 minutes.
2 Blanch the rocket leaves in a little water for 2 minutes. Drain and remove any excess water by patting the rocket dry in a clean tea towel or using paper towels,
3 Tumble the pancetta into the pan and colour – at this point the aroma will be amazing. Add the garlic and stir. Cook gently for a further 5 minutes. Be careful to not burn the garlic as it can easily catch in the hot fat released from the pancetta. Turn off the pan whilst preparing the pasta.
4 Place a large pan of water on to boil. Once boiling, salt well and cook the pasta until *al dente*.
5. Add the rocket to the pan and warm through with the onions. Cook for 4 minutes. Season with the fresh chilli, salt and pepper.
6 Drain the pasta and add it into the sauté pan. Stir and serve with a generous sprinkle of pecorino and some delicate rocket leaves.

CARMELA'S TIPS
If you would like to make the *malfati* by hand, make your egg pasta dough as described on page 13. Roll the dough out into a thin sheet and cut it with a pastry cutter into small shapes of your choice. Alternatively, farfalle would be equally delicious here.

PANCAKE PASTA WITH PESTO

TESTAROLI AL PESTO

Be prepared to try something completely different, a pasta pancake. *Testaroli* are made in the Lunigiana valley area of Tuscany on the border of Liguria. My first experience of them was in a beautiful little restaurant in Pisa; it wasn't a texture I was expecting but I immediately loved the regional character of this dish, made with a loose pancake batter of flour and water, fried into pancakes, sliced into large triangles, then boiled and served with sauce. They're made in large cast iron pans with huge domed lids, which would have been heated over a wood fire. but I use a standard frying pan.

Preparation and chilling time 40 minutes
Cooking time 20 minutes
Serves 4

FOR THE PASTA BATTER
150g semolina flour
   (*semola di grano duro*)
250g '00' flour
Pinch of salt
450ml warm water

FOR THE PESTO
1 large bunch of basil including stalks
50g pine nuts, untoasted
1 garlic clove, peeled
Salt and pepper to season
50g Parmesan, grated (plus extra
   for the table)
Extra virgin olive oil, to obtain
   a dropping consistency

1 Into a bowl, add the semolina flour, '00' flour and salt. Stir to combine.
2 Slowly add in the water and stir — you are looking for a loose pancake batter. Use a fork to ensure any small lumps are removed. Cover and set aside for a minimum of 30 minutes.
3 Place a large pan of water on to boil. Salt well when boiling.
4 Place the basil, pine nuts, garlic, salt, pepper and Parmesan into a food processor and blitz. Slowly add the extra virgin olive oil until you have a loose dropping consistency. Taste and check for seasoning.
5 Add a tablespoon of olive oil to an 18cm frying pan and rub with a little kitchen towel.
6 Spoon in a small ladle of batter and swirl to ensure the batter has coated the bottom of the pan fully. Cook for 2 minutes on each side. Remove and set aside. Repeat until all the batter is used up. Place the pancakes into an oven set at a low temperature to keep warm.
7 Slice the *testaroli* into diamonds or short ribbons.
8 Drop them all into the boiling water and allow to reheat for 2 minutes.
9 Drain and serve the *testaroli* on plates with a drizzle of pesto and an additional grating of Parmesan.

CARMELA'S TIPS
Testaroli can be served with a simple tomato sauce or with browned butter and sage. To make a gluten-free version, use 250g rice flour along with 250ml of water and a pinch of salt.

TORTELLINI FILLED WITH POTATO

TORTELLINI DI PATATE

Everyone loves tortellini. These are filled with delicious soft potato, pancetta and herbs, famous in Mugello, a mountain area near Florence. Potatoes and pasta work so well together. I do think you'll either love or hate the combination though, as it is carb on carb. I've combined the tortellini with a light tomato sauce, but equally a meat sauce or *burro and salvia* (butter and sage) would work too. If you love pasta then you will fall in love with *tortellini di patate*.

Preparation time 1 hour
Cooking time 15 minutes
Serves 4

FOR THE TORTELLINI

400g prepared egg pasta dough (page 13)
Polenta, for dusting

FOR THE FILLING

600g white potatoes, skins on
250g pancetta, thinly sliced
1 banana shallot, peeled and quartered
1 tbsp olive oil
150g Parmesan, grated (plus extra
    for the table)
2 medium eggs
Small bunch of parsley, finely chopped
Salt and pepper to season
Pinch of nutmeg, freshly grated

FOR THE SAUCE

4 tbsp olive oil
2 garlic cloves, peeled and crushed
20 cherry or baby plum tomatoes, halved
2 long tomato vines
1 small chilli, deseeded and finely sliced
Salt and pepper to season
10 fresh basil leaves, roughly torn

1 To make the filling, boil the potatoes with their skins on until tender; retaining the skin stops the potatoes from absorbing too much water. The same technique is used when making potato gnocchi.

2 Put the shallot and pancetta into a food processor and blitz until smooth.

3 Spoon the pancetta and shallot pulp into a small frying pan with 1 tablespoon olive oil and fry off for 3 minutes until lightly coloured. Drain, set aside and allow to cool.

4 Once the potatoes are tender, drain and allow them to cool for a few minutes. Peel them whilst still warm.

5 Rice the potatoes into a bowl. I always use a potato ricer, I find the end result is much better and totally lump-free. Add the pancetta, shallots, Parmesan, eggs, parsley, salt, pepper and nutmeg. Mix well. Taste for additional seasoning.

6 Spoon into a piping bag. Secure at the top and set aside while you prepare the dough. This can be made in advance and left in the fridge.

7 Take the prepared pasta dough and section into two manageable working balls. Roll the dough out using a pasta machine into thin lasagne sheets.

8 Place the sheets on a lightly floured surface. Cut the dough into 4cm squares.

9 Pipe a teaspoonful of the mixture onto the centre of each square. Seal each square (dampen the edges with a little water if required), forming the dough into a triangle.

10 Encourage the filling to stay central to the tortellini and keep the top triangle point horizontal whilst joining the other two corners together. Continue until all of the filling has been used up.

11 Place each tortellini on a little polenta. Allow them to dry for at least an hour before cooking.

12 To make the sauce, take a sauté pan and add the oil and garlic. Fry off over a low heat for 2 minutes.

13 Add the halved tomatoes, vines and chilli. If you have a Parmesan rind pop it in at this stage.

14 Cook over a medium heat for 10 minutes; the tomatoes need to soften. Season with salt and pepper.

15 Place a large pan of water on to boil. Once boiling, salt well and cook the tortellini for around 3 minutes.

16 Check the tomato sauce for seasoning. Just before serving, add the basil and discard the tomato vines.

17 Drain the tortellini and stir them gently into the tomatoes. Serve with extra Parmesan.

UMBRIA

Umbria is landlocked, slap bang in the middle of Italy with no immediate coast, just the Tiber River, which separates the region from Lazio. The region is mountainous and has the most wonderful array of robust dishes to offer. Bordering Tuscany to the west, Le Marche to the east and Lazio to the south of Italy, it's in very good company. Due to the pasturelands, forests and greenery, Umbria feels autumnal and rich. Just thinking about it encourages me to immediately make and eat a bowl of sausages and lentils.

▲ Rose window of Spoleto Cathedral in Umbria.

▶ The Tempio di Santa Maria della Consolazione in Todi, Umbria overlooks a verdant, wide valley.

Perugia is the capital and very beautiful it is too. I stayed in a beautiful *agriturismo* there with my good friend Julie. The onsite restaurant served the most amazing amaretti and pumpkin ravioli I have ever eaten, the kind of meal I never wanted to finish. However, the jewel in the crown is the quaint town of Norcia, famous for hunting wild boar and producing outstanding *capocollo* meat, salami and ham – a wonderland for the pork lover! Umbria boasts beautiful truffles, amazing olive groves and the best black-spotted nut-fed pigs in Italy. The regional pastas are the long strands of pasta made and cut by hand known as *umbricelli* and *ciriole*. It's time to embrace the cuisine of Umbria...

CIRIOLE PASTA WITH A SIMPLE TOMATO SAUCE

CIRIOLE ALLA TERNANA

I recently visited the stunning region of Umbria and on this occasion I spent most of my time in the province of Terni. *Ciriole* is the handmade pasta of Terni and it's still made daily in Narni and Spoleto. It resembles delicate strands of hair and is also known as *umbricelli*. I do love the way that each region has its own take on a pasta shape, confusing us all with yet another name!

Preparation time 1 hour
Cooking time 30 minutes
Serves 4

400g prepared egg pasta dough
   (page 13)
Polenta or semolina, for dusting

FOR THE SAUCE
3 tbsp olive oil
1 medium onion, peeled and
   finely chopped
2 garlic cloves, peeled and crushed
600g fresh, chopped, or tinned tomatoes
Pinch of chilli (optional)
Salt and pepper to season
Small bunch of basil, torn
80g pecorino or Parmesan, grated

1 After allowing the prepared pasta dough to rest for a minimum of 30 minutes, roll the dough out using a rolling pin or pasta machine. Once you have rolled the dough into lasagne sheets, dust with a little flour and fold the sheets over so you can cut the pasta by hand.

2 Cut the pasta into 3mm strands.

3 Place on a tray dusted with a little semolina or polenta.

4 To make the sauce, gently fry off the onion in the olive oil over a medium heat for 5 minutes. Add the garlic and tomatoes. I use fresh tomatoes when they are in season as they are naturally sweeter, but tinned will suffice.

5 Season with a pinch of chilli, if using, and salt and pepper.

6 Scatter over all of the basil, stir and cook for 25 minutes.

7 Place a large pan of water on to boil. Once boiling, salt well. Add the pasta and cook until *al dente*.

8 Drain the pasta and return it to the saucepan. Add the tomato sauce, stir and add half the percorino or Parmesan. Serve with an additional sprinkling of Parmesan.

CARMELA'S TIPS
Any long pasta would work well in this recipe.

PAPPARDELLE WITH A WILD HARE RAGU

PAPPARDELLE ALLA LEPER

A little preparation in advance never hurt anyone, did it? Brining the hare is worth the effort as it tenderises the meat tremendously. If you struggle to find hare, as you possibly may, a good old-fashioned rabbit from your local butchers will do the trick. Legend has said that blood would be used instead of tomatoes in the dish many years ago; thank heavens for ruby red tomatoes! This sauce can be served with any robust pasta, long or short, but paired with pappardelle it becomes a marriage made in heaven. This rich sauce clings beautifully to the wide pasta.

Preparation time 15 minutes
Brining time 24 hours
Cooking time 2 hours 30 minutes
Serves 4

1.3kg hare (or rabbit), jointed
400g pappardelle

FOR THE BRINE
900ml water
80g salt
1 garlic clove, smashed (skin on)
1 red onion, quartered (skin on)
1 sprig rosemary
1 sprig thyme

FOR THE SAUCE
3 tbsp olive oil
1 medium onion, peeled and finely
    chopped
1 garlic clove, peeled and crushed
1 celery stalk, finely chopped
1 carrot, peeled and finely chopped
125ml red wine
1 tbsp tomato purée
1 x 680g bottle passata
100ml water
Pinch of chilli (optional)
Salt and pepper to season
Small handful of celery leaves,
    finely chopped
Small bunch of parsley, roughly chopped
Few basil leaves, torn
80g Parmesan, grated

1 Place the jointed hare in a shallow container.
2 To make the brine, mix the water with the salt and pour it over the hare or rabbit. Add the garlic, quartered onion and sprig of rosemary and thyme.
3 Cover with cling film and place in the fridge for 24 hours.
4 Next prepare the sauce. Into a large shallow pan, pour in the olive oil and tumble in the *soffritto* of onion, garlic, celery and carrot. Fry off for 10 minutes over a medium heat.
5 Drain the hare and pat it dry with some kitchen towel.
6 Place the hare pieces in the pan with the sauce and fry off gently for 10 minutes.
7 Add the red wine, tomato purée, passata and water. Stir.
8 Sprinkle in a little chilli if using, season with salt and pepper and scatter through half the parsley and all of the celery leaves. Cook over a steady low heat for 2 hours.
9 When the hare is tender and cooked through remove it from the pan and de-bone it. Return the meat to the pan and stir. Check for additional seasoning.
10 Cook the pappardelle according to the packet instructions.
11 Drain, retaining a little of the pasta water, and add the pappardelle to the pan with a little of the reserved pasta water.
12 Serve with an additional scattering of parsley and the basil and Parmesan.

CARMELA'S TIPS
The hare would benefit from the full 24-hour brine as I mentioned above, but anything over 12 hours would be fine.

SPAGHETTI WITH SAUSAGE, MUSHROOM AND CREAM SAUCE

SPAGHETTI ALLA NORCINA

This recipe comes from the beautiful town of Norcia situated on the southeasterly side of Umbria. Norcia is best known for its pork, cured meats and truffle. What more could anyone possibly need? This dish has speed to back it up, as well as an autumnal warmth and fantastic flavours too. It's delicious served in a warm bowl with a glass of your favourite vino.

Preparation time 10 minutes
Cooking time 30 minutes
Serves 4

400g dried spaghetti
80g porcini mushrooms
3 tbsp olive oil
1 medium onion, peeled and
    finely chopped
1 garlic clove, peeled and crushed
350g Umbrian sausage
100ml white wine or vermouth
250ml double cream
Pinch of chilli (optional)
½ tsp nutmeg, freshly grated
Salt and pepper to season
Small bunch of basil, torn
80g Parmesan, grated

1 Place the dried porcini in a bowl and cover with boiling water or stock. Allow the mushrooms to rehydrate; this will take approximately 30 minutes.
2 Heat the olive oil in a small shallow pan and fry off the onion and garlic for 3 minutes.
3 Skin the sausages and either roughly chop them, or I prefer to pull rough bite-sized pieces off. Place them in the pan with the onion and garlic and colour all over.
4 Add the white wine and allow to evaporate; this will take a couple of minutes.
5 Reduce the heat and pour in the cream. Stir and keep the pan on a low heat, being careful the cream doesn't catch or burn.
6 Add a pinch of chilli, if using, and the nutmeg and season with salt and pepper.
7 Drain the porcini mushrooms.
8 Chop the mushrooms and add them to the cream sauce. Cook for 15 minutes.
9 Place a large pan of water on to boil. Once boiling, salt well and cook the spaghetti according to the packet instructions until *al dente*.
10 Drain the spaghetti and add the leggy strands to the cream sauce. Toss, sprinkle with a little Parmesan and scatter over a little basil. Serve in warm bowls and enjoy.

CARMELA'S TIPS
The delicious porcini water can be saved and used later. I normally drain the liquid through a little muslin to catch and remove any grit, then simply freeze it or add to stock.

UMBRICELLI WITH PERCH
UMBRICELLI IN SALSA TRASIMENO

These delicate long thin strands of what could easily be mistaken as my daughter Chiara's golden hair are, however, are referred to as 'earth worms'. Beautiful *umbricelli* are handmade and adored in the region of Umbria. Made with a simple blend of flour and water, they are also known as *ciriole*. This dish is a regional speciality and uses freshwater perch.

Preparation time 40 minutes
Cooking time 30 minutes
Serves 4

400g *umbricelli* or any long thin
    pasta strand
3 tbsp olive oil
1 medium shallot, peeled and
    finely chopped
2 garlic cloves, peeled and crushed
1 small carrot, peeled and finely chopped
1 small stick of celery, finely chopped
300g fresh lake perch fillets, de-boned
    and skinned
100ml white wine or vermouth
400g passata
Small bunch of parsley, chopped
A few celery leaves, finely chopped
Pinch of chilli (optional)
Salt and pepper to season
Small bunch of basil, torn
40g Parmesan, grated (optional)

1 Heat the olive oil in a shallow pan and gently fry off the shallot, garlic, carrot and celery for 10 minutes until softened.
2 Break up the perch and add it into the pan. Stir and cook for 2 minutes.
3 Pour in the white wine, stir and reduce for 2 minutes.
4 Add the passata, parsley and celery leaves. Stir, season with chilli, if desired, and salt and pepper.
5 Leave the sauce to cook over a low heat for 30 minutes.
6 Place a large pan of water on to boil. Once boiling, salt well, add the pasta and cook until *al dente*.
7 Drain the pasta, reserving a small ladle of pasta water.
8 Add the pasta into the tomato sauce and stir. Add a little pasta water if required to loosen the pasta a little.
9 Serve and scatter with a little chopped basil and a scattering of Parmesan if desired.

CARMELA'S TIPS
Any long thin pasta will work here. I do love a sprinkle of Parmesan on this dish even though fish is present.

STRANGOZZI PASTA WITH TRUFFLE SAUCE
STRANGOZZI AL TARTUFO

Strangozzi is a slightly thinner version of the well-known tagliatelle we have all come to love and embrace in the UK. It is commonly made over the Christmas period and during certain carnival celebrations too. But in reality we don't need a celebration or festivity to enjoy a bowl of pasta.

---

1 Place a large pan of water on to boil. Once boiling, salt well and cook the pasta until *al dente*.

2 Pour the oil into a small saucepan and add the garlic cloves over a medium heat. Fry the garlic for 5–7 minutes. Once the oil is flavoured, remove the pan from the heat and discard the garlic cloves.

3 Grate the truffle and add it to the warmed oil.

4 Stir and season with salt and pepper.

5 Drain the pasta, reserving 50ml of the cooking water, then return it to the pan with the reserved pasta water.

6 Remove the garlic from the truffle mixture.

7 Stir the truffle mixture through the pasta and serve with a light sprinkling of parsley, and a few shavings of Parmesan if desired.

Preparation time 15 minutes
Cooking time 30 minutes
Serves 4

400g *strangozzi* or tagliatelle
100ml extra virgin olive oil
2 garlic cloves, peeled
100g black truffle, grated
Pinch of salt and pepper
Small bunch of parsley, finely chopped
80g Parmesan, grated (optional)

CARMELA'S TIPS
Make the *strangozzi* by hand as you would make tagliatelle (page 38), and simply make them a little thinner.

VENETO

The beautiful region of Veneto offers a vast and yet diverse landscape, from mountains, sloping steady hills, vast plains stretching for miles, along with a stunning coastline and endless lagoons. Bordering Emilia Romagna, Lombardy, Trentino-Alto Adige, Austria to the north and Friuli to the northeast, Venice is the capital of this romantic region and the type of dishes and style of food has taken its influences very much from the Venetians.

▲ The Rialto fish market, alongside the Grand Canal near the Rialto Bridge, Venice.

▶ Rain mists the surface of a quiet canal in Cannaregio, Venice.

Veneto is a region of rice and polenta, with pasta as a second option. On a recent visit to the capital I enjoyed a variation and different style of cooking. I loved the soft creamy baccala (*baccala mantecato*) nestled on squares of white polenta in the form of *cichetti* along with incredibly fresh fish, seafood and the most fabulous risotto made with *radicchio di Treviso*. My daily visit to the local Rialto market was essential, if not to buy but to enjoy the hustle and bustle, watch the speed of the fishmongers cleaning and preparing the catch of the day, or just smile and walk on by blushing at the whistles of the eighty-five-year-old man perched on his stool. It's a region bursting at its seams with not only beauty and history but the need to discover the real Veneto and the back streets of Venice.

BIGOLI WITH DUCK SAUCE

BIGOLI CON L'ARNA

This recipe usies the Venetian *bigoli* (wholewheat spaghetti) strands of pasta. This dish only calls for a duck carcass and internal duck offal. However, you could boil a small duck and use the meat for a second dish if you prefer. As with other recipes, you could use wholewheat spaghetti or taglietelle here if you are not able to make or buy *bigoli*.

———

Preparation time 15 minutes
Cooking time 1 hour 20 minutes
Serves 4

———

400g *bigoli* or wholewheat spaghetti
Small bunch of parsley, finely chopped
60g Grana Padano, grated

FOR THE STOCK
1 duck carcass (with all offal)
1 medium onion, peeled and quartered
1 large carrot, peeled and halved
2 sticks of celery including
    the leaves, halved
1 large ripe tomato, halved
1 garlic clove, unpeeled
4 sage leaves
65g unsalted butter
Salt and pepper to season

1 In a large saucepan, start by preparing the duck stock. Add the duck carcass to the pan along with the onion, carrot, celery stalks and leaves, tomato and garlic.

2 Top the pan up with water and add a pinch of salt. Boil the duck for around an hour until cooked through. Taste and season the stock if required after an hour.

3 Remove any sinew from the duck offal by just trimming with a small knife. Slice the offal into 3cm pieces. Put the butter into a small sauté pan and add the sage and the duck offal. Cook gently over a medium heat. Add a ladle of the duck stock, place a lid on the pan and simmer for approximately 20 minutes.

4 Once the duck stock is ready, strain through a sieve and discard the vegetables. Check the stock for further seasoning.

5 Bring the duck stock back to the boil and add the *bigoli* pasta to the pan. Cook for 10 minutes until *al dente*.

6 Drain the pasta (reserving the stock). Add the *bigoli* to the offal and and stir, add a little more stock if required.

7 Sprinkle in the chopped parsley, stir and serve with Grana Padano.

BIGOLI WITH SARDINES

BIGOLI IN SALSA

Bigoli hail from the region of Veneto and are still made by hand with passion and a sense of tradition that only the Venetians can do. *Bigoli* are a long thick wholewheat spaghetti but with a rough texture as the dough is pressed through a *torchio* or *bigolaro* press. As you can imagine, I love traditional methods of making pasta and embrace them with my arms fully open. However, you could easily replace the *bigoli* with wholewheat spaghetti.

Preparation time 15 minutes
Cooking time 20 minutes
Serves 4

———

400g *bigoli* or wholewheat spaghetti
8 small fresh sardines
3 tbsp olive oil
2 medium onions, peeled and chopped
   into small cubes
3 tbsp white wine
Salt and pepper to season
Small bunch of parsley, finely chopped
Drizzle of extra virgin olive oil, to finish

1 Rinse the sardines well and remove the bones and innards. Chop into small pieces and set aside.

2 Place a large pan of water on to boil for the pasta. Once boiling, salt well.

3 Pour the olive oil into a sauté pan and add the onions. Bring to a medium heat and cook for 5 minutes. Try to not colour the onions as we want to keep them translucent if possible.

4 Pour in the white wine and stir.

5 Add the sardine pieces and combine. Season with pepper, add half the parsley and stir.

6 Add the *bigoli* to the pan of boiling water and cook until *al dente*.

7 Drain the pasta, reserving a small ladle of pasta water, tumble into the sardines and stir. Add the reserved water and stir until combined. The pasta water will help to emulsify the dish.

8 Sprinkle over the remaining parsley and serve in warm bowls with an extra drizzle of extra virgin olive oil.

CARMELA'S TIPS

You could substitute the white onion for red to add a little colour to the dish, and add fresh thyme to the onions whilst they are cooking gently. At the same time, add a little sprinkle of chilli for additional heat if desired. Once you have the basic dish, it's yours to experiment with for flavour.

———

SQUID INK TAGLIATELLE WITH MANTIS SHRIMPS AND SQUID

TAGLIATELLE AL NERO DI SEPPIE CON CANOCCHIE E CALAMARI

Deep in colour with the aroma of the sea, this dish will unmistakably bring a taste of the ocean to your family table. The pasta can be made by hand as described on page 36 or you can use ready-made squid ink pasta for ease. Now the *canocchie* or 'mantis shrimps' resemble prehistoric creatures from the sea with their firm ridged bodies, delicate legs and beady eyes. If the *canocchie* prove a little tricky to come by, then prawns or scampi make the perfect substitution.

Preparation time 15 minutes
Cooking time 25 minutes
Serves 4

400g pre-prepared cuttlefish ink
    tagliatelle (page 36) or dried
16 *canocchie* or large prawns
3 tbsp olive oil
2 garlic cloves, peeled and finely sliced
1 small chilli, deseeded and
    finely chopped
400g baby plum tomatoes, halved
4 fresh squid, including tentacles,
    bodies cut into 1cm rings
1 large glass white wine
Salt and pepper to season
Small bunch of parsley, chopped

1 Wash the *canocchie* and remove the black digestive tract along the back and the head and gently tease the meat from the shell; this will make eating this dish an absolute pleasure. However, this is entirely up to you. You can simply clean the *canocchie* and just remove the heads.
2 Into a large but shallow sauté pan, pour in the olive oil and bring to a gentle simmer.
3 Add the sliced garlic and chilli and stir with a wooden spoon. Be careful to not burn the garlic as it can catch very easily if left.
4 Tumble in the tomatoes and stir. Squash them with the back of a wooden spoon and cook over a medium heat for 7 minutes.
5 Scatter the squid rings and tentacles into the tomatoes and stir.
6 Add the white wine and reduce by half. Taste and season well with salt and pepper, scatter in half the chopped parsley and stir.
7 Place a large pan of water on to boil. Salt the water once boiling, add the tagliatelle and cook until *al dente*.
8 Add the *canocchie* to the sauce, stir and combine. Cover and cook for 7 minutes. Check for seasoning.
9 Drain the tagliatelle, reserving a ladle of pasta water. Add the tagliatelle and reserved pasta water to the sauce and combine gently. Scatter over the reserved parsley and serve.

CARMELA'S TIPS
Instead of using white wine I often use white vermouth in this recipe.

TAGLIATELLE WITH RABBIT
TAGLIATELLE CON CONIGLIO

Rabbit is incredibly underused in the UK and hard to find. Is it because we tend to see them more as family pets than we do as a meal? I suppose growing up on a farm has helped me grasp the fact they are another source of meat, and very delicious they are too. In Italy and in many European countries, rabbit is widely used and is easy to come by. I'm hoping this will change and it will become a supermarket and butchers' staple. This recipe was given to me by my good friend Monica Cesarato, who is from the Veneto region and loves to cook with this inexpensive meat.

Preparation time 10 minutes
Cooking time 1 hour
Serves 4

400g freshly prepared tagliatelle (page 13) or dried
3 tbsp olive oil
1 carrot, peeled and chopped into small cubes
1 onion, peeled and chopped into small cubes
1 stick celery, chopped into small cubes
1 garlic clove, peeled and finely sliced
1 large glass white wine
450g rabbit meat, off the bone
Salt and pepper to season
2 tbsp tomato purée
300ml vegetable stock
Handful of parsley, chopped
60g Grana Padano, grated

1 Place the olive oil in a saucepan over a low heat and add the chopped carrot, onion and celery. Allow to cook for 10 minutes until softened. Add the garlic and stir. Pour in half the white wine and stir.
2 Roughly portion the rabbit meat, removing the meat from the bone, and add to the pan. Add a pinch of salt, the remaining wine and tomato purée. Allow the wine to evaporate for 2 minutes. Add the stock and cook gently for about 1 hour, covering the pan. If necessary add a little extra water or stock to the pan.
3 Meanwhile, cook the tagliatelle in a large pan of salted boiling water until *al dente*.
4 Drain the tagliatelle, reserving a ladle of pasta water, then add to the pan along with the reserved pasta water and sauté for few minutes.
5 Before serving, add some chopped parsley and a good grind of black pepper.
6 Serve with a sprinkle of Grana Padano cheese.

VENETIAN BEANS WITH PASTA

PASTA E FASIOI

As soon as you tumble beans or pulses into a pasta dish it immediately becomes a bowl of instant comfort. What's even more pleasing in this recipe is that it's not only simple and full of flavour but inexpensive too. The Venetians have a fondness for the *lamon* bean, but this can easily be substituted with cannellini or borlotti beans. I tend to use a small pasta called *ditalini* from Sicily but any small pasta would work equally well.

Preparation time 10 minutes
Cooking time 40 minutes
Serves 4

350g *ditalini* (tiny pasta tubes)
3 tbsp olive oil
350g *guanciale* or pancetta, cut into
    small cubes
1 medium onion, peeled and chopped
    into small cubes
1 medium carrot, peeled and chopped
    into small cubes
1 medium celery stick, chopped into
    small cubes
2 garlic cloves, peeled and crushed
300g dried lamon beans (soaked
    overnight) or 2 x 400g tins cannellini
    or borlotti beans
1 litre meat stock
Salt and pepper to season
Small bunch of parsley, finely chopped
40g Grana Padano, grated

1 If you have managed to search out lamon beans, make sure they have been soaked in water overnight. Drain them and boil in water for approximately 90 minutes.

2 Into a deep-bottomed sauté pan, add the olive oil and fry off the *guanciale* or pancetta gently for 5 minutes.

3 Add the onion, carrot and celery cook gently over a medium heat for around 8 minutes.

4 Add the garlic to the pan and stir.

5 Tumble in the drained beans and combine with the *soffritto* vegetables.

6 Pour in the stock and cook over a medium heat for 20 minutes.

7 Taste and season with salt and pepper and sprinkle in half the chopped parsley.

8 Add the pasta and cook according to the packet instructions, minus 2 minutes to ensure the pasta remains *al dente*.

9 Serve in warm bowls with an additional sprinkle of parsley.

CARMELA'S TIPS

If I have any spare Parmesan or Grana cheese rinds in my fridge I would drop one into the soup when I add the stock. This is optional. I like the flavour, but it is not necessarily in keeping with tradition.

STOCKISTS OF ITALIAN INGREDIENTS AND TOOLS

Below is a list of stockists I have put together to help you find ingredients and products to aid you in your quest for creating mouth-watering and authentic Italian dishes. I use some of these stockists weekly, for example my local Italian deli, but I recommend them all for staple larder goods, fresh fruit, vegetables, regional cured meats, cheeses and more.

___

DELICATESSENS

Foods of Italy
75 Bower Street
Bedford MK40 3RB
www.foodsofitalybedford.co.uk

The Italian Shop (my local delicious deli)
52 Ashburnham Road
Northampton NN1 4QY
www.theitalianshopnorthampton.co.uk

___

Just So Italian
9 Adam & Eve Street
Market Harborough LE16 7LT
www.justsoitalian.co.uk

___

Lina Stores
18 Brewer Street
London W1F 0SH
www.linastores.co.uk

___

The Stony Pantry
1 High Street
Stony Stratford
Bucks MK11 1AA
www.thestonypantry.co.uk

___

Valvona & Crolla
19 Elm Row
Edinburgh EH7 4AA
www.valvonacrolla.co.uk

___

ONLINE STOCKISTS

www.latriestina.co.uk
I'm addicted to their pistachio cream

www.melburyandappleton.co.uk
Larder goods

www.natoora.co.uk
Amazing fresh fruit and vegetables

www.seedsofitaly.com
Grow-your-own seeds and deli goods

www.tenutamarmorelle.com
I love their long-stemmed artichokes

www.valentinafinefoods.com
Various London stores

www.vorrei.co.uk
Incredible cheeses and deli goods

FOR PASTA TOOLS

For pasta tools and gadgets I tend to search the internet but here are three online stores I recommend:

www.amazon.co.uk
General pasta stamps and pins

www.tagliapasta.com
Artisan specialist pasta tools

www.romagnolipastatools.com
Beautifully crafted corzetti stamps and rolling pins from Tuscany